About the Book

In this new acknowledge ... to the most interesting cars of the world, the scope has been extended. Regular readers will find a much wider range of cars covered, and where the author has come across some fascinating but relatively little known model, he has not hesitated to include it. Thus you will find such oddities as a Peugeot estate car adapted to four-wheel drive, one or two cars that are no longer current but still of interest such as the exciting BMW M1, and specialist products like the Avanti II. A representative range of American models is also featured.

The main purpose of the book is to answer the question 'what's that car?', giving instant recognition from the photograph included for every model, and providing all the essential technical data, features and information about it and other models associated with it. However, it also proves fascinating for the enthusiast to browse through, widening his knowledge of, and improving his recognition of, the world's immense variety of cars.

About the Author

... n has been an ..... .or cars of all kinds ever since he had to be forcibly removed from his first 'car', made of sand at the seaside, when he was only 4. Aged 8, he started driving by working the clutch, gear lever and steering from the passenger seat for an understanding aunt who was on essential work and able to get petrol during the war. As a National Service officer he was in charge of a platoon of staff cars and ambulances, and in 1955 went straight from there to the editorial staff of the weekly motoring magazine *The Autocar*.

In 26 years with the magazine he drove and Road Tested all manner of cars, and was Deputy Editor when he left in 1981 to become a freelance motoring and travel writer. His enthusiasm for cars and motoring remains undiminished and he covers all developments in new models and writes Road Tests and other motoring articles for a number of outlets at home and abroad. He has the advantage that he has personal experience of driving most of the cars analysed in this book.

The New Observer's Book of

Automobiles

Compiled by
Stuart Bladon

Frederick Warne

First Edition 1955
Twenty-fifth Edition 1983

NOTE

The specifications contained in this book were collated on the basis of material available to the compiler up to the end of November 1982. All information is subject to change and/or cancellation during the course of the model year. Although every effort has been made to ensure correctness in compiling this book responsibility for inaccuracies and omissions cannot be accepted by the compilers and publishers.

Library of Congress Catalog
Card No. 62–9807

ISBN 0 7232 1641 X

Typeset by CCC, printed and bound in
Great Britain by William Clowes (Beccles) Limited,
Beccles and London

CONTENTS

Ginetta	G.4 Series IV 96
Honda	Accord 97; Prelude 98; Quintet 99
Hyundai	Pony 1400TLS 100
Innocenti	3-Cylindres SE 101
Jaguar	XJ 3.4 102; XJS HE 103
Lada	Niva 104
Lamborghini	Countach 105
Lancia	Delta LX 106; Gamma Olgiata 107; Prisma 108; Trevi 2000 109; Trevi Volumex 110
Land-Rover	County V8 111
Lincoln	Continental 112
Lotus	Eclat Excel 113; Elite Riviera 114; Turbo Esprit 115
Maserati	Biturbo 116; Khamsin 117; Kyalami 118; Merak 119
Mazda	323 1500 GT 120; 929 Coupé 121; RX-7 122
Mercedes-Benz	190E 123; 280TE 124; 300SD 125; 380SEC 126; 500SL 127; 300GD 128
Mercury	Capri 129; Lynx 130; Marquis 131
MG	Metro 132; Metro Turbo 133
Morgan	Plus 8 134
Morris	Ital SLX 135
Oldsmobile	Cutlass Supreme Brougham 136; Delta 88 137; Toronado 138
Opel	Corsa 1.3 139; Manta 1.8 140; Monza 3.0 141
Panther	Kallista 142
Peugeot	104ZS 143; 504 Dangel Break 144; 505 GR Estate Car 145
Plymouth	Reliant Estate Car 146
Pontiac	Firebird Trans Am 147; Grand Prix 148; 6000 Coupé 149
Porsche	911 Turbo 150; 928S 151; 944 152
Range Rover	In Vogue Automatic 153
Reliant	Fox 154; Scimitar GTC 155
Renault	5 Gordini Turbo 156; 9GTL 157; Fuego GTX 158; 30 TX 159
Rolls-Royce	Camargue 160; Corniche 161; Silver Spur 162
Rover	SD Turbo 163; Vitesse 164
Saab	900 GLE 165; 900 Turbo SE 166
Sbarro	Royale 167
Skoda	120LSE 168
Subaru	1800 4WD 169
Suzuki	Alto 170; SJ410Q 171
Talbot	Horizon LD 172; Matra Murena 173; Samba Cabriolet 174; Tagora 2.2 175
Toyota	Celica 2.0 Liftback 176; Corolla 177; Land-Cruiser 178; Supra 179; Tercel 180

Triumph	Acclaim 181
TVR	Tasmin convertible 182
Vauxhall	Astra SR 1600S 183; Cavalier LD 184; Carlton 185
Volkswagen	Golf GLi 186; Passat 187; Polo 188; Santana 189; Scirocco GTi 190
Volvo	360 GLT 191; 760 GLE 192

COUNTRY OF MANUFACTURE

The letter (or letters) following the make of car indicates the country of manufacture. These are:

CH	Switzerland
CS	Czechoslovakia
D	German Federal Republic
E	Spain
F	France
GB	United Kingdom
I	Italy
J	Japan
P	Poland
S	Sweden
SU	Union of Soviet Socialist Republics
USA	United States of America

CARS OF THE WORLD

Over the years since this book first appeared in 1955 there have been numerous editors, and each has endeavoured to make the book more informative and useful. Certainly no reflection against the previous work is intended in enumerating the further improvements made for 1983.

First, it seemed right to take a completely fresh look at the cars which the book should cover. Accordingly I drew up a new list and only afterwards looked at the 1982 edition to see how it compared. The result has been a much wider coverage, with a deliberate aim to include as many of the recently announced cars as possible. At the same time, a lot of the apparent duplication which resulted from covering variants of a model has been avoided.

For example, last year we had three rather similar Rovers, including a repeat of the full mechanical specification for the almost identical 3500SE and Vanden Plas versions. This year there would have been only one—the new SD Turbo diesel. But when, in the closing stages of preparing the material, the new injection version called the Vitesse was announced, it was obviously right for this topical addition to be included.

Obviously we would have to extend the book to something like five times the size (and price!) to be able to include every model on the market; but by being more selective it has been possible to include a good cross-section of the world's cars, including a representative range of American and Japanese products.

Topicality is the key—so don't miss adding next year's edition to your collection in order to keep up to date and be able to refer back for information, because it is likely to be very different from this one.

To the basic format, which is essentially a specification summary, I have endeavoured to add a wider scope of information. A slightly longer 'Identification' section has allowed me to put each car more fully into its proper place, with suitable information to help in correctly identifying the model. At the end, the section previously termed 'Notes' is now 'Features', and where possible I have endeavoured to give a thumbnail sketch of the car, sometimes being rather cruel where I felt this was deserved, as well as drawing attention to significant equipment.

'Autocar' Performance

Cars are dynamic things, and what they do is more important than their basic details; so I felt it was important to include some indication of performance. Of course, we lack the space to go into this in great detail, but by kind permission of the Editor of *Autocar*—my former boss, Ray Hutton—I have been allowed to quote the 0 to 60 mph acceleration time and maximum speed, taken from *Autocar* Road Tests.

Where this data is not available—usually because an up-to-date test was not available at time of closing for press—I have given the manufacturer's claimed figures. In each case this is prefaced by the significant word 'Works' after the 'Performance' sub-heading.

Seeking performance information on American cars I wrote to the various manufacturers, and received a charming letter from one of them stating: 'disappointing news . . . we just do not test our vehicles in this manner'. I am sure that if I was concerned with building refrigerators I would want to know the output, revs and so on of its motor, and I find it astonishing that such basic information is not available from American manufacturers about their cars. However, where no works information was available I have used all other available sources, and in many cases my own experience, to form an estimate of top speed and this is quoted accordingly, making it quite clear that it is an estimate.

My opinion of the 'official' Government fuel consumption figures is fairly low, since the urban cycle is measured on a ludicrous sequence which artificially favours automatics, and the consumption at a mere 55 mph is certainly irrelevant in Europe and, from what I saw of American speeds when I was there, it is so on the other side of the Atlantic as well. However, the consumption at constant 75 mph does give some basis for representative fuel consumption of cars, and is quoted where available. If the figure for 75 mph constant speed is not obtainable, I have tended to quote an actual or estimated overall mpg figure which, in my experience, will not be much different.

For the rest of the information provided, the aim has been to extend it where possible within the space available. Thus you will find information as to whether the disc brakes are internally vented or not, and a little more information about such matters as gear ratios, compression ratio and engine construction.

Finally, I must apologise for any errors you may find. A lot of care has gone into checking the material, but if you do spot a mistake please forgive, and be sure to let me know.

For our American readers

Just because your ancestors forgot how to spell the word 'tyre' on the long and often hazardous voyage across the Atlantic, I do hope you will not hold it against us if this and some other terms in the text seem slightly strange. For example a stabilizer bar in British terminology is an anti-roll bar, and your twin-barrel carburetor will appear here as a twin-choke *carburettor*; and shocks are things you get when playing with the ignition while the engine is running, and nothing to do with the suspension. The term we use here for that suspension item once known as the shock absorber is given with its more correct term 'damper'.

In particular, please note two things: first, the engine power and torque quoted (unless the letters SAE appear) are real figures, measured to the DIN standard. Second, fuel consumption shown as mpg is in miles per Imperial gallon. Please divide by 1.2 to determine how far the car will travel on a US gallon.

I hope you will soon master these little oddities, and that the information the book contains will be a helpful guide to the fascinating variety of cars produced in different parts of the world.

AN EXCITING YEAR

You don't often hear people say nowadays that 'they don't make cars like they used to'. It's generally recognised that immense progress has been made in recent years and that cars are far and away better than before; and this progress in the right direction has been more marked than for a long time past.

Strangely, it has been the incentive of need to improve fuel economy that has been the big motivation in making cars better. It has resulted in cars that are of improved shape, in the interests of better aerodynamics, lighter to give good performance without wasting fuel, and with more useful gear ratios in order to keep engine revs down and again save fuel.

Rapidly the boxey shapes, clumsily big bumpers, and overall impression of bulk and weight generated by the big drive for safety in the 1970s, has given way to more elegant body styles. This is not to suggest that the new generation of cars coming along in the '80s are any less safe; they are probably more so, but it is no longer the prime motivation, and it is not so necessary for the safety factors to be blatantly displayed and clumsily incorporated in the car.

It was with great delight that I went out to Sardinia in July for an advanced view and driving experience of the new Ford Sierra, and I really felt that Ford had made a tremendous stride forward with this new model. It took me a little while to grow accustomed to its very different styling, but with familiarity it soon started to look very right indeed. It is a car that provides a very comfortable ride with its new independent rear suspension, is very easy and relaxing to drive, and has controls, seating, space and finish which all earn extremely high marks. A 1.6L Sierra served me very well on my journey out to the Paris Show, and although there was a very strong headwind all the way down there, it still managed over 30 mpg in fast cruising—a tribute to its good aerodynamic shape.

It's fascinating to see Ford and GM (Vauxhall and Opel) battling so hard in this sector of the market, and no sooner had the Sierra been launched than Vauxhall produced new versions of the Cavalier with engine capacity increased to 1.8-litre size, and with a five-speed gearbox.

GM disappointed me, however, with their new Corsa small car, which I sampled on the flat roads of northern Germany. It struck me as plain inside, disappointingly noisy, and not very certain in its directional stability. However, it could be too early to judge on the basis of the preliminary experience with a prototype, and the Corsa is certainly a very significant new model which is going to be in the news a lot in 1983.

A trend gathering way in Europe, and even, slowly, in Britain, too, is the increased acceptance of diesel engines for cars. The diesel car was given a big fillip during the year by introduction of the very excellent new Rover SD-Turbo and the also very impressive Vauxhall Cavalier and Audi 80 turbodiesel. Driving long journeys in the Rover diesel I felt that in a car able to cruise at 80 mph as well as the SD-Turbo does, the penalties of diesel motoring are now fairly small. The advantages in cost saving become all the more significant as fuel prices rise.

Not least of the advantages is the huge range that the diesel car, equipped with the standard size of tank as for the petrol version, can travel without refuelling. With the Rover SD-Turbo I regularly covered more than 400 miles on a tankful; but with a Citroen CX2500D Safari, motoring rather more gently on holiday in France, I managed over 500 miles on a tankful.

Impressive though these diesel figures were, my greatest mileage in the year without refuelling was 664.2 miles in an RAC-observed run with a Renault 9GTL. It was a demonstration of the Renault 9's extraordinary economy, and although we went fairly slowly we still managed 40 mph average running speed, and went all the way from Calais to Geneva and right round Lake Léman, before running out of fuel on the second circuit of the lake. The results were used by *Autocar* in their 'Dover–Geneva and how far round the lake?' competition, with a Renault 9GTL as first prize.

It all helps to illustrate how economical cars are becoming, and the Renault 9 on this Dover–Geneva run returned 57.66 mpg.

The same influences have greatly improved performance cars, too, and such excellent cars as the BMW 635CSi, the Jaguar XJ-S H.E., and the Mercedes-Benz 500SEC are much more relaxing and rewarding to drive fast, now that they have long-legged gearing.

We certainly should not overlook a significant development of the year—the introduction of the new four-speed economy automatic transmission in the BMW 735i which, for the first time, promised to give better fuel economy than the equivalent manual transmission model.

Another significant development which has come abruptly on to the motoring scene has been the transformation of so many Japanese cars. Once so limited in road behaviour and so dull in appearance, they have taken on attractive new shapes and are much better designed than before. New contenders like the Datsun Stanza and Toyota Supra will make it even harder for importers to keep within agreed quotas.

Far too many new models were launched during the busy motoring year of 1982 to be able to deal with them all here in any detail. But at least you should be able to consult this handy reference book, which I hope will stay always with you, so that you can study their statistics and main features.

FORD (GB, D) ┃ COVER CAR ┃ Sierra XR4

Identity: Special high performance version of the Sierra with aerodynamic body enhanced by twin spoilers at rear. Standard engine is 2.8 litre V6 with fuel injection, and five-speed gearbox. Long list of special equipment included. Three-door body.

Engine: Front-mounted V6-cylinder with fuel injection. Cast iron block and heads; breakerless electronic ignition. Bore, 93 mm, stroke 68.5 mm; capacity 2,792 cc. Power, 147 bhp (110 kW) at 5,700 rpm; torque: no data available at time of closing for press.

Transmission: Rear-wheel drive; five-speed manual gearbox standard, no automatic version available. Final drive ratio 3.36-to-1. Top gear mph at 1,000 rpm: 24.1.

Suspension: Front, independent, MacPherson struts; coil springs and gas-filled telescopic dampers. Anti-roll bar. Rear, independent, semi-trailing arms, coil springs and gas filled telescopic dampers. Anti-roll bar.

Steering: Rack and pinion, power assistance optional.

Brakes: Vented discs front, drums rear, servo-assisted.

Tyres: 195/60 VR 14.

Dimensions: Length 4394 mm (173 in.), width 1720 mm (67.7 in.), height 1361 mm (53.6 in.), wheelbase 2609 mm (102.7 in.).

Unladen weight: 1174 kg (2588 lb).

Performance (Works): Maximum speed, 125 mph. (No acceleration or fuel consumption data available on closing for press).

Features: Impressive blend of performance, comfort and sporting appeal. Bi-plane tail fin treatment reduces aerodynamic coefficient to 0.32. Progressive rate springs. Special seats; distinctive alloy wheels.

Identity: Two-seater two-door mid-engined coupé in very limited production with glass fibre bodywork and fixed top; now sold direct from works.

Engine: Mid-mounted Ford V6-cylinder with Weber carburettor. Bore, 93.7 mm, stroke 72.4 mm; capacity 2994 cc. Power, 136 bhp (102 kW) at 5000 rpm; torque 167 lb ft (235 Nm) at 3000 rpm.

Transmission: Rear-wheel drive; five-speed manual gearbox; no automatic option; 3.17-to-1 final drive. Top gear mph at 1,000 rpm: 25.6.

Suspension: Front, independent, wishbones and coil springs, telescopic dampers, anti-roll bar. Rear, independent, wishbones and coil springs, telescopic dampers, anti-roll bar.

Steering: Rack and pinion.

Brakes: Discs front and rear, servo-assisted.

Tyres: 195/60 HR 14, 7 in rim.

Dimensions: Length 3990 mm (157 in), width 1650 mm (65 in), height 1140 mm (45 in), wheelbase 2300 mm (90.5 in).

Unladen weight: 1085 kg (2390 lb).

Performance: Maximum speed, 120 mph. 0 to 60 mph, 8.5 sec. Fuel consumption, 26.9 mpg (at constant 75 mph).

Features: High performance, quick steering, good cornering but a little twitchy on directional stability at speed.

ALFA ROMEO (I)　　SC 1.5 Alfasud Cloverleaf

Identity: Newly available in 1982 in five-door form. Compact hatchback with sporting handling, but with standard 1.3-litre engine is a little under-powered; better response with Cloverleaf version, which has 1.5-litre engine standard. Also available with three doors.

Engine: Front-mounted four-cylinder with cylinders horizontally opposed. Ohc each side with toothed belt drive. Bore, 84 mm, stroke 67.2 mm; capacity 1490 cc. Power, 95 bhp (71 kW) at 5,800 rpm; torque 96 lb ft (133 Nm) at 4,000 rpm.

Transmission: Front-wheel drive; five-speed gearbox standard (no automatic option). Hypoid bevel final drive. Top gear mph at 1,000 rpm: 17.9.

Suspension: Front, independent, MacPherson struts; coil springs and telescopic dampers. Anti-roll bar. Rear, dead beam axle on longitudinal links and Panhard rod; coil springs and telescopic dampers.

Steering: Rack and pinion.

Brakes: Discs front and rear, servo-assisted.

Tyres: 165/70 SR 13.

Dimensions: Length 3978 mm (157 in), width 1616 mm (63.4 in), height 1370 mm (53.9 in), wheelbase 2455 mm (96.7 in).

Unladen weight: 925 kg (2040 lb).

Performance (Works): Maximum speed, 106 mph. 0 to 60 mph, 10.7 sec. Fuel consumption, 34.4 mpg (at constant 75 mph).

Features: Full instrumentation. Digital clock. Adjustable steering column. Wood rim steering wheel. Headlamp wash/wipe.

ALFA ROMEO (I)   GTV6

Identity: Sporting coupé, much improved when turned into the GTV6 by fitting the V6 2.5-litre Alfa engine in December 1980. Suspension was revised at the same time, and new moulded front and rear body sections incorporate a deep spoiler at the front. Note the power bulge on the bonnet.

Engine: Front-mounted V6-cylinder with ohc each bank, driven by toothed belt, and pushrod operation for exhaust valves. Bosch L-Jetronic fuel injection, and breakerless ignition. Bore, 88 mm, stroke 68.3 mm; capcity 2492 cc. Power, 160 bhp (119 kW) at 5,600 rpm; torque 157 lb ft (217 Nm) at 4,000 rpm.

Transmission: Rear-wheel drive; five-speed gearbox standard. No automatic option. Hypoid bevel final drive, 4.1-to-1. Top gear mph at 1,000 rpm: 22.0.

Suspension: Front, independent, wishbones and longitudinal torsion bars. Telescopic dampers. Anti-roll bar. Rear, De Dion layout with Watts linkage; coil springs and telescopic dampers. Anti-roll bar.

Steering: Rack and pinion.

Brakes: Vented discs front, discs rear, servo-assisted.

Tyres: 195/60 HR 15.

Dimensions: Length 4260 mm (168 in), width 1664 mm (65.5 in), height 1331 mm (52.4 in), wheelbase 2400 mm (94.5 in).

Unladen weight: 1227 kg (2702 lb).

Performance: Maximum speed, 130 mph. 0 to 60 mph, 8.8 sec. Fuel consumption, 28.6 mpg (at constant 75 mph).

Features: Sliding steel panel sunroof standard; alloy wheels; metallic paint. Electric front windows. Radio/cassette with stereo on both. Wood rim steering wheel.

ALFA ROMEO (I)   1.5 Sprint Veloce

Identity: Attractively styled hatchback version of Alfasud, with two doors and opening rear window, with spoiler on tail just beneath. Look for later model's identifying *veloce* script on door following 1982 changes, also a waistline paint stripe and broad flash along the sides between the wheel arches.

Engine: Front-mounted four-cylinder with cylinders horizontally opposed. Ohc each side with toothed belt drive. Bore, 84 mm, stroke 67.2 mm; capacity 1490 cc. Power, 95 bhp (71 kW) at 5,800 rpm; torque 96 lb ft (133 Nm) at 4000 rpm.

Transmission: Front-wheel drive; five-speed gearbox standard (no automatic option). Hypoid bevel final drive. Top gear mph at 1,000 rpm: 17.9.

Suspension: Front, independent, MacPherson struts; coil springs and telescopic dampers. Anti-roll bar. Rear, dead beam axle on longitudinal Watts linkage, with Panhard rod; coil springs and telescopic dampers.

Steering: Rack and pinion.

Brakes: Discs front and rear, servo-assisted.

Tyres: 165/70 SR 13.

Dimensions: Length 4020 mm (158 in), width 1620 mm (64 in), height 1306 mm (51.4 in), wheelbase 2455 mm (96.7 in).

Unladen weight: 925 kg (2040 lb).

Performance (Works): Maximum speed, 109 mph. 0 to 60 mph, 10.2 sec. Fuel consumption, 35.3 mpg (at constant 75 mph).

Features: Distinctive alloy wheels. Features light in boot and under bonnet, but not the headlamp wash/wipe system as on Cloverleaf, since front has four round halogen headlamps.

ALPINE RENAULT (F)

Identity: Two-seater high performance coupé with glass fibre body and Renault V6 engine. First launched 1971; V6 version followed 1976. Two-door with opening rear window.

Engine: Rear-mounted V6-cylinder with all-aluminium construction. Single ohc for each bank of cylinders. Bore, 88 mm, stroke 72 mm; capacity 2664 cc. Power, 148 bhp (110.5 kW) at 6000 rpm; torque 148 lb ft (204 Nm) at 3500 rpm.

Transmission: Rear-wheel drive; five-speed manual gearbox; all ratios indirect. Final drive 3.44-to-1. Top gear mph at 1000 rpm: 23.1.

Suspension: Front, independent, coil springs and wishbones; telescopic dampers. Anti-roll bar. Rear, independent, coil springs and wishbones; telescopic dampers. Anti-roll bar.

Steering: Rack and pinion.

Brakes: Vented discs front and rear, servo-assisted.

Tyres: 220/55 VR 365.

Dimensions: Length 4250 mm (167 in), width 1650 mm (65 in), height 1150 mm (45 in), wheelbase 2270 mm (89.3 in).

Unladen weight: 1040 kg (2292 lb).

Performance (Works): Maximum speed, 140 mph. 0 to 60 mph, 7.8 sec. Fuel consumption, 32.5 mpg (at constant 75 mph).

Features: Aerodynamic body shape, with headlamps behind sloping transparent covers. Spoiler beneath bumper. Alloy wheels.

Identity: Compact AMC car with choice of four-door saloon or estate car body. Saloon available in base or DL versions; estate car has DL or Limited trim packs. Standard engine 4.2-litre six with higher compression.

Engine: Front-mounted six-cylinder with hydraulic tappets, twin-choke downdraught carburettor. Closed loop catalytic system; unleaded fuel. Bore, 95.3 mm, stroke 99 mm; capacity 4230 cc. Power (SAE): 120 bhp (90 kW) at 3500 rpm; torque 206 lb ft (285 Nm) at 1,800 rpm.

Transmission: Rear-wheel drive; four-speed gearbox standard. Five-speed manual, or three-speed automatic are options. Top gear mph at 1,000 rpm: 31.1.

Suspension: Front, independent, wishbones with twin ball joints, strut rod on lower arm; coil springs and telescopic dampers. Anti-roll bar. Rear, live axle on semi-elliptic leaf springs; telescopic dampers.

Steering: Recirculating ball; power assistance optional.

Brakes: Vented discs front, drums rear, servo-assisted.

Tyres: 195/75 R 14.

Dimensions: Length 4648 mm (185 in), width 1803 mm (71 in), height 1292 mm (50.9 in), wheelbase 2743 mm (108 in).

Unladen weight: 1325 kg (2921 lb).

Performance (Works): Maximum speed, 103 mph. Fuel consumption, 17 mpg (estimated).

Features: Vinyl roof on saloon; bucket seats, woodgrain instrument panel. Digital clock. Engine has fuel feed-back system and knock sensor for more efficiency. Air conditioning, power windows and door locks are among options.

AMERICAN MOTORS (USA)   Eagle

Identity: Choice of liftback, four-door saloon and four-door estate car, all with four-wheel drive. Normal drive is to rear wheels; front drive added at touch of facia switch. 2.5-litre engine standard, with four-speed gearbox; six-cylinder optional.

Engine: Front-mounted four-cylinder with side camshaft, hydraulic tappets. Carter twin-choke carb. Unleaded fuel. Bore, 101.6 mm, stroke 76.2 mm; capacity 2471 cc. Power, 88 bhp (65.5 kW) at 4000 rpm; torque 231 lb ft (167 Nm) at 2800 rpm.

Transmission: Four-wheel drive; four-speed manual gearbox standard; five-speed manual or three-speed automatic are options. Top gear mph at 1,000 rpm: 31.5.

Suspension: Front, independent, wishbones and coil springs; telescopic dampers. Anti-roll bar. Rear, live axle on semi-elliptic leaf springs; telescopic dampers. Anti-roll bar optional.

Steering: Recirculating ball, power assisted.

Brakes: Vented discs front, drums rear, servo-assisted.

Tyres: 195/75 R 15.

Dimensions: Length 4740 mm (186.6 in), width 1825 mm (71.8 in), height 1410 mm (55.5 in), wheelbase 2780 mm (109.4 in).

Unladen weight: Liftback, 1378 kg (3038 lb); estate, 1490 kg (3284 lb).

Performance (est.): Maximum speed, 87 mph. Fuel consumption, 17 mpg.

Features: Power steering and glass-belted radial tyres are standard. DL models have reclining seats, woodgrain facia, styled wheel covers and other detail refinements. Roof rack is available.

AMERICAN MOTORS (USA)   Spirit GT

Identity: New for 1983, additional version of Spirit, as sporty variant. Spirit is available only as two-door liftback four-seater. Six-cylinder 4.2-litre engine now standard.

Engine: Front-mounted six-cylinder with compression raised to 9.2-to-1. Hydraulic tappets. Bore, 94.3 mm, stroke 99.1 mm; capacity 4228 cc. Power (SAE): 117 bhp (87 kW) at 3500 rpm; torque 231 lb ft (167 Nm) at 2000 rpm.

Transmission: Rear-wheel drive; choice of five-speed manual (option), three-speed automatic, or standard four-speed manual. Top gear mph at 1000 rpm: 23.2.

Suspension: Front, independent, wishbones and coil springs. Telescopic dampers. Anti-roll bar. Rear, live axle on semi-elliptic leaf springs. Telescopic dampers.

Steering: Recirculating ball; power assistance optional.

Brakes: Vented discs front, drums rear, servo-assisted.

Tyres: P195/70 R 14.

Dimensions: Length 4242 mm (167 in), width 1829 mm (72 in), height 1308 mm (51.5 in), wheelbase 2438 mm (96 in).

Unladen weight: 1275 kg (2809 lb).

Performance (est.): Maximum speed, 95 mph. Fuel consumption, 18 mpg (at constant 75 mph).

Features: Good range of standard equipment including alloy wheels and fog lamps; power window lifts and door locks (optional). Rear spoiler is also an option, as is electric tailgate release.

ASTON MARTIN (GB)   Lagonda V8

Identity: Impressive luxury saloon with Aston Martin V8 engine. Extensive use of alumunium for body panels; separate steel chassis. An immensely satisfying car to drive; very fast, very safe, and magnificent on long journeys.

Engine: Front-mounted V8-cylinder with twin ohc each bank. Alloy for block and heads; wet cylinder liners. Four Weber carbs. Bore, 100 mm, stroke 85 mm; capacity 5340 cc. Power and torque: no figures quoted by Aston Martin.

Transmission: Rear-wheel drive; Chrysler Torqueflite automatic transmission standard (no manual version available). Top gear mph at 1,000 rpm: 25.8

Suspension: Front, independent, coil springs and wishbones; telescopic dampers. Anti-roll bar. Rear, De Dion layout, with coil springs and telescopic dampers.

Steering: Rack and pinion, power assisted.

Brakes: Ventilated discs front and rear, servo-assisted.

Tyres: 235/70 VR 15.

Dimensions: Length 5820 mm (208 in), width 1790 mm (70.5 in), height 1300 mm (51 in), wheelbase 2910 mm (115 in).

Unladen weight: 2023 kg (4459 lb).

Performance: Maximum speed, 143 mph. 0 to 60 mph, 8.8 sec. Fuel consumption, 17.6 mpg (at constant 75 mph).

Features: Lavish equipment including electric front window lifts, air conditioning, and automatic locking of whole car 15 sec after removing key from ignition. Digital instruments. Pop-up headlamps.

ASTON MARTIN (GB) V8 Volante

Identity: Special convertible version of the V8, introduced mid-1978. Note the way in which the tail is higher, in comparison with the tapering tail of the saloon. Fabulously expensive but very impressive. Aluminium body on separate steel chassis.

Engine: Front-mounted V8-cylinder with twin ohc each bank, chain driven; all alloy construction. 4-choke Weber carb. Bore, 100 mm, stroke 85 mm; capacity 5341 cc. No power or torque figures quoted by Aston Martin, but power probably in the region of 300 bhp.

Transmission: Rear-wheel drive; five-speed ZF gearbox or Chrysler Torqueflite automatic transmission. Limited slip diff. Manual, 3.54-to-1; automatic 3.07. Top gear mph at 1,000 rpm: 26.0.

Suspension: Front, independent, wishbones and coil springs; telescopic dampers. Anti-roll bar. Rear, De Dion axle with Watts linkage and longitudinal arms; adjustable telescopic dampers.

Steering: Rack and pinion, power assisted.

Brakes: Vented discs front and rear, servo-assisted.

Tyres: GR 70 VR 15.

Dimensions: Length 4665 mm (183.7 in), width 1830 mm (72 in), height 1325 mm (52 in), wheelbase 2610 mm (103 in).

Unladen weight: 1780 kg (3924 lb).

Performance: Maximum speed, 146 mph. 0 to 60 mph, 6.6 sec. Fuel consumption, 18.4 mpg (at constant 75 mph).

Features: Rather noisy but magnificent response; slight body movement with hood down but not sufficient to spoil driving enjoyment. Superb equipment, leather upholstery, and air conditioning all standard.

AUDI (D)

Identity: Impressive top version of Audi 80 range, with generous equipment, and powered by the 1.9-litre five-cylinder engine. A fast and refined car, very compact and manageable, with outstanding fuel economy.

Engine: Front-mounted five-cylinder with belt-driven ohc. Solex carb. Compression 10-to-1. Bore, 79.5 mm, stroke 77.4 mm; capacity 1921 cc. Power, 113 bhp (84.5 kW) at 5,900 rpm; torque 111 lb ft (154 Nm) at 3700 rpm.

Transmission: Front-wheel drive; five-speed (4 + E) gearbox; three-speed automatic available. Top gear mph at 1000 rpm: 25.2.

Suspension: Front, independent, MacPherson struts; coil springs and telescopic dampers. Anti-roll bar. Rear, dead beam axle on trailing arms and Panhard rod; coil springs and telescopic dampers. Anti-roll bar.

Steering: Rack and pinion, power assisted.

Brakes: Discs front, drums rear, servo-assisted.

Tyres: 185/60 HR 14.

Dimensions: Length 4385 mm (172.5 in), width 1680 mm (66 in), height 1365 mm (54 in), wheelbase 2535 mm (100 in).

Unladen weight: 1000 kg (2201 lb).

Performance (Works): Maximum speed, 112 mph. 0 to 60 mph, 10.3 sec. Fuel consumption, 29.4 mpg (at constant 75 mph).

Features: Pressure jet headlamp washers, sunroof, central locking and electric window lifts. Clean, distinguished four-door saloon body with large boot. Special alloy wheels.

Identity: Striking new saloon with exceptionally aerodynamic three-box saloon body. Flush-fitting glass, and extensive attention to similar detail points to reduce drag, giving factor of 0.30. Five-cylinder 2.2-litre (detailed below) or 1.9-litre engines. Some markets also get 1.8-litre four-cylinder and 2.0-litre diesel.

Engine: Front-mounted five-cylinder with mechanical fuel injection. Single ohc; alloy head. Bore, 79.5 mm, stroke 86.4 mm; capacity 2144 cc. Power, 136 bhp (100 kW) at 5700 rpm; torque 130 lb ft (180 Nm) at 4,800 rpm.

Transmission: Front-wheel drive; five-speed gearbox (designated 4 + E) standard; three-speed automatic optional. Top gear mph at 1,000 rpm: 27.7.

Suspension: Front, independent, MacPherson struts, coil springs and telescopic dampers; anti-roll bar. Rear, semi-independent, trailing arms and torsion beam axle; coil springs and telescopic dampers. Torsion beam axle gives anti-roll effect.

Steering: Rack and pinion, power assisted.

Brakes: Vented discs front, solid discs rear, servo-assisted.

Tyres: 185/70 HR 15.

Dimensions: Length 4793 mm (188.7 in), width 1814 mm (71.4 in), height 1422 mm (56 in), wheelbase 2687 mm (105.8 in).

Unladen weight: 1210 kg (2668 lb).

Performance (Works): Maximum speed, 124 mph. 0 to 60 mph, 10.3 sec. Fuel consumption, 36.2 mpg (at constant 75 mph).

Features: Very comfortably furnished and exceptionally well-equipped in this top of the range CD version. Less fully equipped CS version also available. ABS anti-lock brake system optional.

AUDI (D)

Identity: First introduced with 1.9-litre engine, the striking Audi Coupé, sister car to the Quattro, went up in engine size to 2.2-litre in additional model introduced Paris 1982, launched in Britain in November. Rear spoiler, alloy wheels and single lens headlamps identify new model.

Engine: Front-mounted five-cylinder with Bosch K-Jetronic fuel injection. Belt-driven ohc. Compression ratio 9.3-to-1. Bore, 79.5 mm, stroke 86.4 mm; capacity 2,144 cc. Power, 130 bhp (97 kW) at 5,900 rpm; torque 126 lb ft (171 Nm) at 4,800 rpm.

Transmission: Front-wheel drive; five-speed close-ratio gearbox standard—no automatic option. Top gear mph at 1,000 rpm: 20.8.

Suspension: Front, independent, MacPherson struts; coil springs and telescopic dampers. Anti-roll bar. Rear, dead beam axle on trailing links with Panhard rod; coil springs and telescopic dampers.

Steering: Rack and pinion, power assisted.

Brakes: Vented discs front, solid discs rear, servo-assisted.

Tyres: 185/60 HR 14.

Dimensions: Length 4348 mm (171.2 in), width 1681 mm (66.2 in), height 1389 mm (54.7 in), wheelbase 2537 mm (99.9 in).

Unladen weight: 1048 kg (2310 lb).

Performance (Works): Maximum speed, 122 mph. 0 to 60 mph, 9.1 sec. Fuel consumption, 34.0 mpg (at constant 75 mph).

Features: Delightfully smooth and responsive car to drive. Generous equipment including sun roof, central locking, rear wash/wipe, headlamp washers and interior adjustable mirrors all standard.

AUDI (D)

Identity: Audi's trend-setting, rally-winning coupé with four-wheel drive. Identifiable from ordinary fwd coupé by presence of the wheel arch fairings which the coupé does not have.

Engine: Front-mounted five-cylinder with belt-driven ohc, Bosch electronic ignition, and KKK turbocharger. Iron block, alloy head. Bore, 79.5 mm, stroke 86.4 mm; capacity 2214 cc. Power, 200 bhp (149 kW) at 5,500 rpm; torque 210 lb ft (290 Nm) at 3,500 rpm.

Transmission: Four-wheel drive; five-speed manual gearbox, and hypoid final drive at each end. Both diffs lockable for tackling extreme conditions such as snow, mud or sand. Top gear mph at 1,000 rpm: 23.6.

Suspension: Front, independent, MacPherson struts; coil springs and telescopic dampers. Anti-roll bar. Rear, independent, MacPherson struts and coil springs. Telescopic dampers. Anti-roll bar.

Steering: Rack and pinion; power assistance standard.

Brakes: Discs front and rear, servo-assisted.

Tyres: 205/60 VR 15.

Dimensions: Length 4404 mm (173 in), width 1723 mm (68 in), height 1344 mm (53 in), wheelbase 2524 mm (99.4 in).

Unladen weight: 1264 kg (2786 lb).

Performance: Maximum speed, 135 mph. 0 to 60 mph, 7.3 sec. Fuel consumption, 27.1 mpg (at constant 75 mph).

Features: Phenomenal performance due to the unrivalled traction of four-wheel drive. Smooth and tremendously responsive engine. Remarkable handling up to certain prescribed limits, but some care needed in exploring beyond the adhesion extremes.

AUSTIN (GB)   Ambassador 2.0 HL

Identity: Replacement for former Princess, with many improvements including redesign of body as a five-door hatchback. Available as 1.7 with L or HL trim, 2.0HL (data follows), and two twin carb. 2.0 versions—HLS and luxury Vanden Plas model.

Engine: Front-mounted four-cylinder with single ohc; engine positioned transversely; alloy head; single SU carb. Bore, 84.5 mm, stroke 89 mm; capacity 1994 cc. Power, 92 bhp (69 kW) at 4,900 rpm; torque 114 lb ft (158 Nm) at 2,750 rpm.

Transmission: Front-wheel drive; four-speed manual gearbox; helical spur final drive, 3.48-to-1. Automatic three-speed transmission available. Top gear mph at 1,000 rpm: 20.4.

Suspension: Front, independent, wishbones and Hydragas spring and damper units, linked to rear suspension on same side, giving anti-roll effect. Rear, independent, trailing arms and Hydragas spring and damper units inter-linked with front.

Steering: Rack and pinion, with optional power assistance.

Brakes: Discs front, drums rear, servo-assisted.

Tyres: 185/70 HR 14.

Dimensions: Length 4550 mm (179 in), width 1760 mm (69.4 in), height 1400 mm (55 in), wheelbase 2670 mm (105 in).

Unladen weight: 1263 kg (2784 lb).

Performance: Maximum speed, 100 mph. 0 to 60 mph, 14.3 sec. Fuel consumption, 31.2 mpg (at constant 75 mph).

Features: Spacious car with semi-estate car load carrying ability; exceptionally comfortable ride; sealed battery and 12,000-mile service interval.

Identity: Special luxury version of Metro introduced 1982 with traditional Vanden Plas interior embellishments. Two-door hatchback body; look for Vanden Plas badges (VP merged) each side on rear quarter, and waist level coachlines.

Engine: Front-mounted four-cylinder with pushrod ohv; compression 9.4-to-1. Engine mounted transversely, with transmission in sump. Bore, 70.6 mm, stroke 81.3 mm; capacity 1275 cc. Power, 60 bhp (45 kW) at 5,250 rpm; torque 69 lb ft (95 Nm) at 3,200 rpm.

Transmission: Front-wheel drive; four-speed gearbox; surprisingly there is no automatic option. Ratio 3.44-to-1. Top gear mph at 1000 rpm: 17.2.

Suspension: Front, independent, unequal length links; bottom link braced by anti-roll bar; Hydragas springs and telescopic dampers. Rear, independent, connected side to side; trailing arms; Hydragas springs with coil spring pre-load; internal damping in Hydragas unit.

Steering: Rack and pinion.

Brakes: Discs front, drums rear, servo-assisted.

Tyres: 155/70-12.

Dimensions: Length 3405 mm (134 in), width 1549 mm (60.9 in), height 1361 mm (53.6 in), wheelbase 2251 mm (88.6 in).

Unladen weight: 769 kg (1695 lb).

Performance: Maximum speed, 94 mph. 0 to 60 mph, 13.5 sec. Fuel consumption, 37.9 mpg (at constant 75 mph).

Features: Polished walnut trim inside, thick pile woven velvet seat upholstery, and many touches of extra quality and refinement for those who are prepared to pay extra for a better finished car.

AUSTIN (GB)   Mini Mayfair

Identity: A better-equipped version of the Mini. Similar to Mini City, with Economy 1.0-litre engine.

Engine: Front-mounted four-cylinder with pushrod ohv; cast iron head and block. Transverse installation. SU carb. Bore, 64.6 mm, stroke 76.2 mm; capacity 998 cc. Power, 39 bhp (29 kW) at 4750 rpm; torque 51 lb ft (70.5 Nm) at 2000 rpm.

Transmission: Front-wheel drive; four-speed manual gearbox in engine sump. Final drive 3.44-to-1. Top gear mph at 1000 rpm: 15.9.

Suspension: Front, independent, wishbones and rubber cone springs; telescopic dampers. Rear, independent, trailing arms and rubber cone springs; telescopic dampers.

Steering: Rack and pinion.

Brakes: Drums front and rear, servo-assisted.

Tyres: 145 SR 10.

Dimensions: Length 3055 mm (120.3 in), width 1410 mm (55.5 in), height 1346 mm (53.0 in), wheelbase 2037 mm (80.2 in).

Unladen weight: 615.5 kg (1357 lb).

Performance: Maximum speed, 86 mph. 0 to 60 mph, 17.5 sec. Fuel consumption, 60.5 mpg (at constant 56 mph).

Features: Most luxurious Mini ever, with Raschelle cloth trim, cut-pile carpet, tinted glass, radio and passenger door mirror standard. As an extra, alloy wheels and wider tyres, with wheel arch extensions, are available.

AUTOBIANCHI (I)   A112 Abarth

Identity: Small Italian car of sporting character, sadly not imported to Britain. Chunky, two-door hatchback body. Several versions of Autobianchi are available, starting with the Junior; Abarth is the performance model with tuned engine.

Engine: Front-mounted four-cylinder with alloy head, chain-driven side camshaft and pushrods. Weber twin-choke carb, 10.4-to-1 compression. Bore, 67.2 mm, stroke 74 mm; capacity 1049 cc. Power, 69 bhp (51.5 kW) at 6,600 rpm; torque 119 lb ft (86 Nm) at 4,200 rpm.

Transmission: Front-wheel drive; four-speed gearbox standard; five-speed optional. Top gear mph at 1,000 rpm: 16.8.

Suspension: Front, independent, MacPherson struts and coil springs; telescopic dampers. Anti-roll bar. Rear, independent, wishbones and transverse leaf spring; telescopic dampers.

Steering: Rack and pinion.

Brakes: Discs front, drums rear, servo-assisted.

Tyres: 155/70 SR 13.

Dimensions: Length 3230 mm (127 in), width 1480 mm (58 in), height 1360 mm (53.5 in), wheelbase 2040 mm (80.3 in).

Unladen weight: 700 kg (1543 lb).

Performance (Works): Maximum speed, 99 mph. 0 to 60 mph, 12.3 sec. Fuel consumption, 36.2 mpg (at constant 75 mph).

Features: Slightly basic interior trim, but car is well engineered and has sporting appeal, with extra instruments and alloy wheels in this top version. Crisp handling and tidy steering.

AVANTI (USA) Avanti II

Identity: Small production American four-seater two-door coupé with distinctive styling; glass fibre body on perimeter chassis of steel. Hand-built, each taking 14 weeks to build. Also available ex-factory as reconditioned secondhand units.

Engine: Front-mounted V8-cylinder Chevrolet unit with hydraulic tappets. Bore, 94.9 mm, stroke 88.4 mm; capacity 5001 cc. Power (SAE): 150 bhp (112 kW) at 3,800 rpm; torque 236 lb ft (326 Nm) at 2,400 rpm.

Transmission: Rear-wheel drive; GM Hydra-Matic automatic (no manual transmission version available), with three ratios plus overdrive. Exceptionally high gearing. Twin traction limited slip diff. Top gear mph at 1,000 rpm: 34.4.

Suspension: Front, independent, wishbones and coil springs; telescopic dampers. Anti-roll bar. Rear, live axle on semi-elliptic leaf springs; telescopic dampers. Anti-roll bar.

Steering: Rack and pinion, servo-assisted.

Brakes: Discs front, drums rear, servo-assisted.

Tyres: 205/75 R 15.

Dimensions: Length 4902 mm (193 in), width 1788 mm (70.4 in), height 1382 mm (54.4 in), wheelbase 2769 mm (109 in).

Unladen weight: 1621 kg (3570 lb).

Performance (Works): Maximum speed, 109 mph. Fuel consumption, 15 mpg (at constant 75 mph).

Features: Wide range of equipment available including special wheels, 'moon' roof, and Recaro seats. Air conditioning standard.

BENTLEY (GB)   Mulsanne Turbo

Identity: Special high performance version of the Mulsanne saloon, introduced Geneva, 1982. Chief identity feature is the painted radiator grille surround, unlike chromed surround of standard Mulsanne.

Engine: Front-mounted V8-cylinder with all-aluminium construction, hydraulic tappets, cast iron cylinder liners. Turbo unit blows through enclosed carburettor. Bore, 104 mm, stroke 99 mm; capacity 6750 cc. No power or torque figures are quoted by Rolls-Royce for their engines.

Transmission: Rear-wheel drive; GM Hydraulic automatic transmission with Rolls-Royce adaptations, and electric column-mounted selector control. Top gear mph at 1000 rpm: 26.2.

Suspension: Front, independent, wishbones and coil springs; telescopic dampers. Anti-roll bar. Rear, independent, semi-trailing arms and coil springs; telescopic dampers. Automatic self-levelling. Anti-roll bar.

Steering: Rack and pinion, power assisted.

Brakes: Vented discs front, solid discs rear, servo-assisted.

Tyres: 235/70 HR 15.

Dimensions: Length 5310 mm (248 in), width 1890 mm (74.4 in), height 1490 mm (59 in), wheelbase 3060 mm (120 in).

Unladen weight: 2270 kg (5005 lb).

Performance: Maximum speed, 135 mph. 0 to 60 mph, 10.0 sec. Fuel consumption, 16.1 mpg (at constant 75 mph).

Features: Superb quality of finish, unequalled by any other car in the world, and in this version with the added appeal of terrific acceleration. Air conditioning, electric windows and so on all standard.

BMW (D)

Identity: Revised body and major engineering changes introduced in Germany November 1982, and in Britain early 1983 as two-door only; more rounded front but traditional BMW double-oval grille and four lamps. Choice of four-cyl. 1.8-litre engine (316, 318i), or six-cyl. 2-litre or 2.3.

Engine: Front-mounted six-cylinder with belt driven single ohc and inclined valves in hemi-head. Bosch L-Jetronic injection. Compression ratio 9.8-to-1. Bore, 80 mm, stroke 76.8 mm; capacity 2316 cc. Power, 139 bhp (102 kW) at 5,300 rpm; torque 148 lb ft. (205 Nm) at 4,000 rpm.

Transmission: Rear-wheel drive; five-speed manual gearbox standard. Three-speed automatic optional. Final drive ratio 3.25-to-1. Top gear mph at 1,000 rpm: 25.4.

Suspension: Front, independent, MacPherson struts; coil springs and telescopic dampers. Anti-roll bar. Rear, independent, semi-trailing arms; coil springs and telescopic dampers. Anti-roll bar.

Steering: Rack and pinion, power assistance optional.

Brakes: Vented disc front, solid discs rear, servo-assisted. Anti-lock brake system (ABS) optional.

Tyres: 195/60 VR 14.

Dimensions: Length 4325 mm (170 in), width 1645 mm (64.8 in), height 1380 mm (54.3 in), wheelbase 2570 mm (101 in).

Unladen weight: 1080 kg (2380 lb).

Performance (Works): Maximum speed, 126 mph. 0 to 60 mph, 9.2 sec. Fuel consumption, 34.5 mpg (at constant 75 mph).

Features: Attractive combination of sporting handling and responsive performance, with comfort and high safety standard. Bonnet swept up in front of windscreen. Spoiler on boot. Alloy wheels.

BMW (D)

Identity: Although apparently similar to the old model, new version of 528i introduced mid-1981 is substantially re-bodied and brought a wide range of improvements.

Engine: Front-mounted straight six-cylinder with single ohc and Bosch electronic fuel injection. Cast iron block, alloy head. Bore, 86 mm, stroke 80 mm; capacity 2788 cc. Power, 184 bhp (137 kW) at 5800 rpm; torque 177 lb ft (244 Nm) at 4,200 rpm.

Transmission: Rear-wheel drive; five-speed manual gearbox standard; three-speed automatic optional. Hypoid final drive, ratio 3.45-to-1. Top gear mph at 1,000 rpm: 25.6.

Suspension: Front, independent, MacPherson struts and double links; coil springs and telescopic dampers; anti-roll bar. Rear, independent, semi-trailing arms and coil springs. Special auxiliary linkages to prevent toe-out in severe cornering. Telescopic dampers.

Steering: ZF recirculating ball; power assistance standard.

Brakes: Discs front and rear, servo-assisted. Anti-lock brake system available.

Tyres: 165/70 VR 14.

Dimensions: Length 4620 mm (182 in), width 1699 mm (67 in), height 1415 mm (55.7 in), wheelbase 2624 mm (103 in).

Unladen weight: 1408 kg (3101 lb).

Performance: Maximum speed, 133 mph. 0 to 60 mph, 8.8 sec. Fuel consumption, 31.4 mpg (at constant 75 mph).

Features: Sporting handling, very smooth engine; a rewarding car for the enthusiast driver who must have a saloon. High level of equipment, with electric window lifts and central locking. Air conditioning and electric sunroof available.

Identity: Revised version of Bavarian two-door coupé, visually much the same (spoiler on the boot lid and front air dam identify the new model), but extensively revised and improved to make this a most impressive high performance car. Service indicator to show when maintenance is needed, and suspension modifications as on Series 5.

Engine: Front-mounted six-cylinder with single ohc, driven by chain. Alloy head, cast iron block. Bosch L-Jetronic fuel injection with Motronic electronic control of injection and ignition. Bore, 92 mm, stroke 86 mm; capacity 3,430 cc. Power, 218 bhp (163 kW) at 5,200 rpm; torque 224 lb ft (310 Nm) at 4,000 rpm.

Transmission: Rear-wheel drive; five-speed manual gearbox; hypoid bevel final drive, 3.07-to-1. Automatic is no-cost option. Top gear mph at 1,000 rpm: 28.9.

Suspension: Front, independent, MacPherson struts; coil springs and telescopic dampers. Anti-roll bar. Rear, independent, semi-trailing arms with wheel control links; coil springs and telescopic dampers. Anti-roll bar.

Steering: ZF ball and nut, power assisted.

Brakes: Vented discs front, solid discs rear, servo-assisted.

Tyres: 220/55 VR 390.

Dimensions: Length 4755 mm (187 in), width 1725 mm (68 in), height 1365 mm (53.7 in), wheelbase 2626 mm (103.4 in).

Unladen weight: 1442 kg (3175 lb).

Performance: Maximum speed, 139 mph (fourth). 0 to 60 mph, 7.3 sec. Fuel consumption, 32.1 mpg (at constant 75 mph).

Features: Lavishly equipped, but there are some extras such as air conditioning and heated seats. Comprehensive instrumentation includes fuel consumption gauge, service indicator, check control panel and trip computer.

BMW (D)

RRX 386Y

Identity: In Britain, this is the top model of the 7-Series BMW range, though in Germany there is also the 745i, with turbocharged engine. Detail improvements announced October 1982 include revised radiator grille and electric driving seat adjustment with 'memory'.

Engine: Front-mounted six-cylinder with chain-driven single ohc. Alloy head. Engine capacity slightly reduced in 1982, and compression increased to 10-to-1. Bore, 92 mm, stroke 86 mm; capacity 3,430 cc. power, 218 bhp (163 kW) at 5,200 rpm; torque 224 lb ft. (310 Nm) at 4000 rpm.

Transmission: Rear-wheel drive; five-speed manual gearbox or four-speed automatic, with anti-slip torque converter brake. Top gear mph at 1000 rpm: 33.1 (automatic).

Suspension: Front, independent, MacPherson struts; coil springs and telescopic dampers. Anti-roll bar. Rear, independent, semi-trailing arms with extra wheel-control linkages as 528i. Coil springs and telescopic dampers.

Steering: ZF recirculating ball, power assisted.

Brakes: Vented discs front, solid discs rear, servo-assisted.

Tyres: 205/70 HR 14.

Dimensions: Length 4859 mm (191.3 in), width 1801 mm (70.9 in), height 1430 mm (56.3 in), wheelbase 2794 mm (110 in).

Unladen weight: 1530 kg (3374 lb).

Performance (Works): Maximum speed, 132 mph. 0 to 60 mph, 7.7 sec. Fuel consumption, 28.8 mpg (at constant 75 mph).

Features: Superbly finished and lavishly equipped car in new and even more refined form. New automatic transmission claimed to give better fuel economy than manual five-speed version. Alloy wheels.

BMW (D)

Identity: Fabulous mid-engined two-door coupé, seen at first for some years as a prime show exhibit, and then made familiar in the hands of GP drivers (Pro Car series), and put on ordinary retail market. Spectacularly fast, yet fully road-equipped.

Engine: Mid-mounted six-cylinder with twin ohc driven by chain, and Kugelfischer fuel injection. Breakerless ignition. Four valves per cylinder. Bore, 93.4 mm; stroke 84 mm; capacity 3,453 cc. Power, 277 bhp (207 kW) at 6,500 rpm; torque 239 lb ft (330 Nm) at 5,000 rpm.

Transmission: Rear-wheel drive; five-speed gearbox by ZF. Hypoid bevel final drive with limited slip diff. Top gear mph at 1,000 rpm: 24.3.

Suspension: Front, independent, wishbones and coil springs; telescopic dampers; anti-roll bar. Rear, independent, wishbones and coil springs; telescopic dampers; anti-roll bar.

Steering: Rack and pinion.

Brakes: Vented discs front and rear, servo-assisted.

Tyres: 205/55bVR 16 front; 225/50 VR 16 rear.

Dimensions: Length 4360 mm (172 in), width 1820 mm (72 in), height 1140 mm (45 in), wheelbase 2560 mm (100.8 in).

Unladen weight: 1418 kg (3122 lb).

Performance: Maximum speed, 162 mph. 0 to 60 mph, 5.5 sec. Fuel consumption, 17.0 mpg (overall).

Features: Pop-up headlamps, glass fibre body; multi-tubular chassis. Fabulous road grip and very high safety standards in brakes, steering, directional stability and cornering. Made only in left-hand drive, and production ceased.

BRISTOL (GB)   Beaufighter

Identity: Introduced January 1980, this special version of the 412/S3 comes as cabriolet, and has turbocharged engine.

Engine: Front-mounted V8-cylinder with hydraulic tappets, Carter carburettor, and turbocharger. Bore, 101.6 mm, stroke 91 mm; capacity 5898 cc. No figures quoted for power and torque.

Transmission: Rear-wheel drive; Chrysler Torqueflite automatic transmission—no manual version available. Limited slip diff. Choice of 3.07-to-1 or 2.88 final drive ratio. Top gear mph at 1,000 rpm: 26.0.

Suspension: Front, independent, wishbones and coil springs; telescopic dampers. Anti-roll bar. Rear, live axle on longitudinal links, Watts linkage, and torsion bars; self-levelling provision.

Steering: Recirculating ball, power assisted.

Brakes: Discs front and rear, servo-assisted.

Tyres: 225/70 VR 15.

Dimensions: Length 4940 mm (194.5 in), width 1765 mm (69.5 in), height 1447 mm (57 in), wheelbase 2895 mm (114 in).

Unladen weight: 1750 kg (3858 lb).

Performance (Works): Maximum speed, 140 mph. 0 to 60 mph, 7.0 sec. Fuel consumption, 15.7 mpg (touring).

Features: Open car motoring combined with good performance and hand-built coachwork and nice touches of luxury in the interior fittings. Zagato-designed body, built largely in aluminium.

BRISTOL (GB)   **Brigand**

Identity: New version of former 603/S2 model, introduced Birmingham 1982. Two-door four-seater body much as before, and main difference is that the 5.9-litre V8 engine is now turbocharged. Well-made and engineered; traditional vintage 'feel'.

Engine: Front-mounted V8-cylinder with Bristol-developed turbocharger. Hydraulic tappets. Carter four-choke carb. Bore, 101.6 mm, stroke 91 mm; capacity 5898 cc. No figures quoted for power and torque.

Transmission: Rear-wheel drive; Chrysler Torqueflite three-speed automatic transmission (no manual version available). Final drive 2.88-to-1, or 3.07. Limited slip diff. Top gear mph at 1000 rpm: 28.6.

Suspension: Front, independent, wishbones and coil springs; adjustable telescopic dampers. Anti-roll bar. Rear, live axle on longitudinal arms and Watts linkage; torsion bars and adjustable telescopic dampers.

Steering: ZF recirculating ball, power assisted.

Brakes: Discs front and rear, servo-assisted.

Tyres: 215/70 VR 15.

Dimensions: Length 5910 mm (193 in), width 1770 mm (69.6 in), height 1430 mm (56.3 in), wheelbase 2900 mm (114 in).

Unladen weight: 1746 kg (3850 lb).

Performance (Works): Maximum speed, 150 mph. Fuel consumption 14 mpg (overall).

Features: Well-appointed saloon with quality interior furnishings and generous equipment including electric seat adjustment; leather upholstery and walnut facia. Alloy wheels.

BUICK (USA)   Century Custom Coupé

Identity: Two-door saloon version of Buick Century range; others are Sedan, Limited Coupé and Limited Sedan. Sedan versions have four doors. All-new range launched for 1982 model year.

Engine: Front-mounted four-cylinder with electronic fuel injection. 3-litre V6 and 4.3-litre V6 diesel are options. Bore, 101.6 mm, stroke 76.2 mm; capacity 2475 cc. Power, 90 bhp (67 kW) at 4,000 rpm; torque 134 lb ft (185 Nm) at 2,400 rpm.

Transmission: Front-wheel drive; three-speed automatic standard, with high final drive ratio of 2.39-to-1. Top gear mph at 1,000 rpm: 29.6

Suspension: Front, independent, MacPherson struts and coil springs; telescopic dampers. Anti-roll bar. Rear, live axle on longitudinal links with Panhard rod and coil springs; telescopic dampers. Self-levelling available.

Steering: Rack and pinion; power assistance standard.

Brakes: Vented discs front, drums rear, servo-assisted.

Tyres: 185/80 R13.

Dimensions: Length 4805 mm (189 in), width 1720 mm (68 in), height 1360 mm (53.5 in), wheelbase 2665 mm (105 in).

Unladen weight: 1215 kg (2676 lb).

Performance (Works): Maximum speed, 96 mph. Fuel consumption, 30 mpg (EPA).

Features: Distinguished appearance with thought to aerodynamic considerations. Velour seat upholstery and seat-mounted console. Facia in simulated leather.

BUICK (USA)

Identity: Luxury model available in saloon or coupé versions of the Limited or Park Avenue models; there is also an Estate Car variant. Base engine is 4.1-litre V6, but there are also 5-litre V8 petrol and 5.7-litre V8 diesel available.

Engine: Front-mounted V6-cylinder with hydraulic tappets; Rochester carb. Breakerless ignition. Bore, 100.7 mm, stroke 86.4 mm; capacity 4128 cc. Power (SAE): 125 bhp (93.5 kW) at 4,000 rpm; torque 129 lb ft (178 Nm) at 2,000 rpm.

Transmission: Rear-wheel drive; Hydra-Matic automatic three-speed transmission with overdrive; column-mounted selector. Top gear mph at 1,000 rpm: 24.7.

Suspension: Front, independent, wishbones and coil springs; telescopic dampers. Anti-roll bar. Rear, live axle on longitudinal links with upper links on to differential. Coil springs and telescopic dampers. Anti-roll bar optional.

Steering: Recirculating ball steering, power assisted.

Brakes: Vented discs front, drums rear, servo-assisted.

Tyres: 215/75 R 15.

Dimensions: Length 5660 mm (222.8 in), width 1930 mm (76 in), height 1465 mm (57.7 in), wheelbase 3020 mm (119 in).

Unladen weight: 1725 kg (3803 lb).

Performance (est.): Maximum speed, 95 mph. Fuel consumption, 16 mpg (overall).

Features: Tilt steering column, remote boot release, central locking, and six-way seat adjustment for which 'memory' provision is available. Cruise control.

BUICK (USA)   Regal Sport Coupé

Identity: Big-selling line, to which the Regal Estate Wagon was added for 1982. Also available are the Coupé and saloon versions of the Regal and Regal Limited, plus the Regal Sport Coupé. Standard engine is 3.8-litre V6; also available are 4.1-litre V6, and two diesels (4.3-litre V6 and 5.7-litre V8).

Engine: Front-mounted V6-cylinder with hydraulic tappets; Rochester carb. Electronic ignition. Garrett turbocharger. Bore, 96.5 mm, stroke 86.3 mm; capacity 3791 cc. Power (SAE): 174 bhp (130 kW) at 4,000 rpm; torque 270 lb ft (373 Nm) at 2,600 rpm.

Transmission: Rear-wheel drive; Hydra-Matic automatic transmission, three-speed plus overdrive. Final drive 3.08-to-1. Top gear mph at 1,000 rpm: 23.3.

Suspension: Front, independent, wishbones and coil springs; telescopic dampers. Anti-roll bar. Rear, live axle on longitudinal arms with links on to top of diff. Coil springs and telescopic dampers. Anti-roll bar optional.

Steering: Recirculating ball, power assisted.

Brakes: Vented discs front, drums rear, servo-assisted.

Tyres: 185/75 SR 14.

Dimensions: Length 5095 mm (200.6 in), width 1815 mm (71.5 in), height 1380 mm (54.3 in), wheelbase 2745 mm (108 in).

Unladen weight: 1480 kg (3263 lb).

Performance (est.): Maximum speed, 114 mph. Fuel consumption, 15 mpg (overall).

Features: Electronic climate control system. Simulated convertible body, but top is fixed. Small oblong vertical rear quarter windows.

BUICK (USA)

Identity: Introduced in Europe at Paris 1982. American version of the GM 'J' car, with front drive and transverse engine. This is the smallest car exported by GM. Four-door saloon body with sloping front, recessed oblong lamps, and wide grille.

Engine: Front-mounted four-cylinder with alloy head and single belt-drive ohc. Rochester twin-choke carb. Transverse mounting. Bore, 89 mm, stroke 80 mm; capacity 1991 cc. Power, 90 bhp (67 kW) at 5,100 rpm; torque 109 lb ft (151 Nm) at 2700 rpm.

Transmission: Rear-wheel drive; five-speed manual gearbox; three-speed automatic optional. Top gear mph at 1000 rpm: 20.0.

Suspension: Front, independent, MacPherson struts; coil springs and telescopic dampers. Anti-roll bar. Rear, semi-independent, torsion beam axle on trailing arms; coil springs and telescopic dampers. Anti-roll bar optional.

Steering: Rack and pinion; power assistance optional.

Brakes: Vented discs front, drums rear, servo-assisted.

Tyres: 195/70 R 13.

Dimensions: Length 4450 mm (175 in), width 1690 mm (66.5 in), height 137.5 mm (54 in), wheelbase 2570 mm (160 in).

Unladen weight: 1115 kg (2458 lb).

Performance (est.): Maximum speed, 97 mph. Fuel consumption, 23 mpg (overall).

Features: Large range of optional equipment, and fairly comprehensive standard feature list including such items as imitation wire wheel trims for wheels, radio and centre console.

BUICK (USA)

Identity: Compact car available as two-door coupé or four-door saloon; big glass area, rather slabby front. Electronic fuel injection through single injector in carburettor position introduced 1982. Base engine is 2.5-litre; 2.8-litre V6 available.

Engine: Front-mounted four-cylinder with hydraulic tappets, and engine mounted transversely. Side camshaft, pushrods and rockers. Bore, 101.6 mm, stroke 76.2 mm; capacity 2471 cc. Power, 90 bhp (67 kW) at 4,000 rpm; torque 132 lb ft (182 Nm) at 2,400 rpm.

Transmission: front-wheel drive; four-speed manual gearbox. Three-speed automatic available. Top gear mph at 1,000 rpm: 21.4.

Suspension: Front, independent, wishbones and coil springs; telescopic dampers. Anti-roll bar. Rear, dead beam axle on longitudinal links with Panhard rod; coil springs and telescopic dampers.

Steering: Rack and pinion, power assisted.

Brakes: Vented discs front, drums rear, servo-assisted.

Tyres: 185/80 R 13.

Dimensions: Length 4600 mm (181 in), width 1750 mm (69 in), height 1365 mm (53.7 in), wheelbase 2665 mm (104.9 in).

Unladen weight: 1160 kg (2557 lb).

Performance (Works): Maximum speed, 96 mph. Fuel consumption, 20.2 mpg (at constant 75 mph).

Features: Felt knit cloth upholstery. Cruise control available with manual or automatic versions. Low rolling resistance tyres available. Four-door model is the Skylark Limited Sedan.

CADILLAC (USA)   Cimarron

Identity: Four-door saloon, with optional luggage grid on boot lid. Fog lamps below bumper identify 1983 model. 2-litre engine has fuel injection standard—as on all '83 Cadillacs. Vertically slatted grille is another indentifying feature of the 1983 model (previously horizontal ribbing).

Engine: Front-mounted four-cylinder with side camshaft, pushrods and hydraulic tappets. Electronic fuel injection. Compression 9.3-to-1. Bore, 92 mm, stroke 74 mm; capacity 1983 cc. Power (SAE): 86 bhp (64 kW) at 4,900 rpm; torque 110 lb ft (149 Nm) at 2,400 rpm.

Transmission: Front-wheel drive; five-speed manual gearbox standard. Automatic three-speed transmission optional. Top gear mph at 1,000 rpm: 31.4.

Suspension: Front, independent, MacPherson struts; coil springs and telescopic dampers. Anti-roll bar. Rear, independent, semi-trailing arms and coil springs; telescopic dampers. Anti-roll bar.

Steering: Rack and pinion, servo-assisted.

Brakes: Vented discs front, drums rear, servo-assisted.

Tyres: 195/70 R 13.

Dimensions: Length 4397 mm (173 in), width 1652 mm (65 in), height 1321 mm (52 in), wheelbase 2571 mm (101 in).

Unladen weight: 1197 kg (2639 lb).

Performance (est.): Maximum speed, 102 mph. Fuel consumption, 24 mpg (overall).

Features: Perforated leather-trimmed seats. Large circular speedo. and rev. counter. Three-spoke leather-trimmed wheel.

CADILLAC (USA) Fleetwood Brougham Coupé

Identity: Grand example of the 'big is beautiful' concept of the American car, often despised in Europe, but still admired in America. Simulated convertible body style, and two-door body; Coupé and Sedan De Villes, and Fleetwood Brougham Coupé, Sedan and Limousine all with similar styling.

Engine: Front-mounted V8-cylinder with alloy heads; central camshaft working valves by hydraulic tappets. Compression 8.5-to-1. Digital fuel injection. Bore, 88 mm, stroke 84 mm; capacity 4087 cc. Power (SAE): 135 bhp (101 kW) at 4,400 rpm; torque 200 lb ft (277 Nm) at 2200 rpm.

Transmission: Rear-wheel drive; Hydra-Matic automatic transmission with overdrive. Top gear mph at 1,000 rpm: 34.9.

Suspension: Front, independent, wishbones and coil springs; telescopic dampers. Anti-roll bar. Rear, live axle on longitudinal links and upper links to diff. Coil springs and telescopic dampers. Pneumatic self-levelling optional.

Steering: Varying ratio recirculating ball, power assisted.

Brakes: Vented discs front, drums rear, servo-assisted.

Tyres: 215/75 R 15.

Dimensions: Length 5614 mm (221 in), width 1914 mm (75.4 in), height 1387 mm (54.6 in), wheelbase 3085 mm (121.5 in).

Unladen weight: 1808 kg (3986 lb).

Performance (est.): Maximum speed, 110 mph. Fuel consumption, 16 mpg (overall).

Features: Electronic climate control and fuel data panel. Headlamp, wiper and cruise control switches on separate panel. Knit fabric upholstery.

CADILLAC (USA) Seville Elegante diesel

Identity: Luxury limousine style model, introduced 1980, continues for 1983 with new front grille (Cadillac name plate in corner of grille identifies latest model). Details given below for diesel engine which is optional on all except Fleetwood Limousine and Cimarron. Standard engine is 4.1-litre petrol V8, fuel injected.

Engine: Front-mounted V8-cylinder with special 'water in fuel' detector for injection system. Hydraulic tappets; alloy head. Bore, 103.1 mm, stroke 86 mm; capacity 5737 cc. Power. 105 bhp (78 kW) at 3,200 rpm; torque 196 lb ft (271 Nm) at 1,600 rpm.

Transmission: Rear-wheel drive; Hydra-Matic three-speed automatic transmission, with column control. Top gear mph at 1,000 rpm: 32.3.

Suspension: Front, independent, wishbones and coil springs; telescopic dampers. Anti-roll bar. Rear, live axle on longitudinal links, with upper links on to differential. Telescopic dampers, with self-levelling provision.

Steering: Varying ratio recirculating ball, power assisted.

Brakes: Vented discs front, drums rear, servo-assisted.

Tyres: 215/75 R 15.

Dimensions: Length 5202 mm (204.8 in), width 1801 mm (71 in), height 1379 mm (54.3 in), wheelbase 2895 mm (114 in).

Unladen weight: 2014 kg (4440 lb).

Performance (est.): Maximum speed, 91 mph. Fuel consumption 19 mpg (overall).

Features: Front seats separated by centre console with integral fold-down centre armrest. Leather seat upholstery. Simulated teak facia panel. Digital instruments.

CATERHAM CARS (GB)   Super Seven

Identity: Originally the Lotus Super Seven, but Caterham Cars of Surrey, England, took over the manufacturing rights, and the little two-seater sports car lives on in three forms: TC, GT, and GT Sprint. Decidedly basic weather protection, but tremendous fun.

Engine: Front-mounted four-cylinder with twin ohc. Two Dellorto carbs. Compression 10.3-to-1. Bore, 81.0 mm, stroke 77.6 mm; capacity 1599 cc. Power, 120 bhp (90 kW) at 6,300 rpm; torque 107 lb ft (148 Nm) at 5,300 rpm.

Transmission: Rear-wheel drive; four-speed close ratio gearbox, with short travel change. Final drive 3.64-to-1. Top gear mph at 1,000 rpm: 18.6.

Suspension: Front, independent, wishbones and coil springs; telescopic dampers. Anti-roll bar. Rear, live axle on A-bracket, with trailing arms; coil springs and telescopic dampers.

Steering: Rack and pinion; 2.7 turns lock-to-lock.

Brakes: Discs front, drums rear, servo-assisted.

Tyres: 165 HR 13.

Dimensions: Length 3403 mm (134 in), width 1587 mm (62.5 in), height 1104 mm (43.5 in), wheelbase 2235 mm (88.0 in).

Unladen weight: 527 kg (1162 lb).

Performance: Maximum speed, 114 mph. 0 to 60 mph, 6.2 sec. Fuel consumption, 28.3 mpg (overall).

Features: Terrific performance. Very direct steering and phenomenal roadholding. Detachable sidescreens and button-on hood. The nearest thing to a motor cycle with four wheels.

CHEVROLET (USA)

Camaro Z28

Identity: Model name dates back to 1967, and appeal continues similar but with much altered body style. Three models available: Sport Coupé, Grand Touring Berlinetta, and the performance version, Z28. Sport Coupé has 2.5-litre 4-cyl.; Berlinetta gets 2.8-litre V6.

Engine: Front-mounted V8-cylinder with fuel injection. Compression 9.5-to-1. Bore, 94.9 mm, stroke 88.4 mm; capacity 5001 cc. Power (SAE): 165 bhp (123 kW) at 4,200 rpm; torque 240 lb ft (332 Nm) at 2,400 rpm.

Transmission: Rear-wheel drive; four-speed manual gearbox or three-speed automatic optional. Final drive ratio 3.23-to-1. Top gear mph at 1000 rpm: 23.2

Suspension: Front, independent, MacPherson struts and (separate) coil springs; telescopic dampers. Anti-roll bar. Rear, live axle on longitudinal links with Panhard rod; coil springs and telescopic dampers.

Steering: Recirculating ball steering, power assisted.

Brakes: Discs front, drums rear, servo-assisted (all-disc brakes optional).

Tyres: 205/70 R 14.

Dimensions: Length 4770 mm (187.8 in), width 1850 mm (73 in), height 1270 mm (50 in), wheelbase 2565 mm (101 in).

Unladen weight: 1415 kg (3120 lb).

Performance (est.): Maximum speed, 121 mph. Fuel consumption, 16 mpg (overall).

Features: Aircraft-style interior, with console housing glove box and selected controls. Optional air conditioning. Six-way power seat adjustment. Rear seat backrest folds for extra luggage space.

CHEVROLET (USA)   Celebrity

Identity: Family saloon with same wheelbase as Citation, but almost a foot longer, yet still shorter and lighter than Malibu. Second generation fwd Chevrolet, offering improvements in ride and handling. Two- and four-door saloons, with three trim levels.

Engine: Front-mounted four-cylinder with hydraulic tappets. Compression 8.2-to-1. Electronic fuel injection. Transverse mounting. Bore, 101.6 mm, stroke 76.2 mm; capacity 2,471 cc. Power, 90 bhp (67 kW) at 4,000 rpm; torque 134 lb ft (185 Nm) at 2400 rpm.

Transmission: Front-wheel drive; three-speed automatic transmission, with column-mounted selector. Top gear mph at 1000 rpm: 25.0.

Suspension: Front, independent, MacPherson struts; coil springs and telescopic dampers. Anti-roll bar. Rear, torsion beam axle on longitudinal links; Panhard rod; coil springs and telescopic dampers.

Steering: Rack and pinion, power assisted.

Brakes: Vented discs front, drums rear, servo-assisted.

Tyres: 205/70 R 13.

Dimensions: Length 4783 mm (188.3 in), width 1745 mm (68.7 in), height 1365 mm (53.7 in), wheelbase 2665 mm (104.9 in).

Unladen weight: 1240 kg (2734 lb).

Performance (est.): Maximum speed, 95 mph. Fuel consumption, 22 mpg (overall).

Features: Special attention to interior noise levels, with extra insulation for optional 4.3-litre diesel. Other engine option is 2.8-litre V6. Air conditioning optional.

CHEVROLET (USA) Corvette

Identity: Claimed to be the 'most-collected' sports car in America, Corvette has been in production in various forms since 1953. Two-seater GT with high-back seats and (optional) opening wrap-round rear window. Pop-up headlamps and sleek, low-drag body of glass fibre.

Engine: Front-mounted V8-cylinder with electronic fuel injection, named Cross-Fire Injection. Bore, 101.6 mm, stroke 88.4 mm; capacity 5736 cc. Power (SAE): 200 bhp (149 kW) at 4,200 rpm; torque 285 lb ft (394 Nm) at 2,800 rpm.

Transmission: Rear-wheel drive; automatic three-speed transmission plus overdrive standard. Torque converter brake to prevent fuel-wasting slip. Top gear mph at 1000 rpm: 29.0.

Suspension: Front, independent, wishbones and coil springs; telescopic dampers. Anti-roll bar. Rear, independent, two trailing arms each side and transverse links; coil springs and telescopic dampers. Optional anti-roll bar.

Steering: Recirculating ball, power assisted.

Brakes: Vented discs front and rear, servo-assisted.

Tyres: 255/60 R 15.

Dimensions: Length 4705 mm (185.2 in), width 1755 mm (69 in), height 1230 mm (48.4 in), wheelbase 2490 mm (98 in).

Unladen weight: 1550 kg (3417 lb).

Performance (est.): Maximum speed, 130 mph. Fuel consumption, 16 mpg (overall).

Features: Special high-quality paint finish, in choice of 12 colours. Available extras include opening frameless glass hatch with remote release, and special alloy wheels; also solar screen glass roof panels.

CHEVROLET (USA)　　Malibu Classic Wagon

Identity: Estate car version of the big Malibu; Classic vehicle is also available as four-door six-seater saloon, and is basis for the Monte Carlo coupé. V6 3.8-litre engine standard; options are 5.7-litre diesel (detailed below) and 4.4- or 5-litre V8 petrol.

Engine: Front-mounted V8-cylinder with central camshaft, chain driven. Compression 22.5-to-1. Bore, 103 mm, stroke 86 mm; capacity 5737 cc. Power, 105 bhp (78 kW) at 3,200 rpm; torque 200 lb ft (277Nm) at 1600 rpm.

Transmission: Rear-wheel drive; Hydra-Matic automatic transmission standard. Selector control on column. Top gear mph at 1000 rpm: 35.5.

Suspension: Front, independent, wishbones and coil springs; telescopic dampers. Anti-roll bar. Rear, live axle on longitudinal links, with upper links on to diff. Coil springs and telescopic dampers. Anti-roll bar optional.

Steering: Recirculating ball, servo-assisted.

Brakes: Vented discs front, drums rear, servo-assisted.

Tyres: 195/75 SR 14.

Dimensions: Length 4890 mm (192.5 in), width 1835 mm (72.2 in), height 1410 mm (55.5 in), wheelbase 2745 mm (108 in).

Unladen weight: 1670 kg (3682 lb).

Performance (est.): Maximum speed, 90 mph. Fuel consumption, 18 mpg (at constant 75 mph).

Features: Huge carrying capacity. Rectangular headlamps and new grille as Caprice for 1983 model. Fabric upholstery; simulated wood grain facia.

CHEVROLET (USA)   Monte Carlo

Identity: Coupé version of the Malibu saloon, with two doors and small window on rear quarter each side. Standard engine is 3.6-litre V6; 4.3-litre V6 diesel and 4.4-litre V8 petrol optional (detailed below).

Engine: Front-mounted V8-cylinder with twin-choke Rochester carb. Compression 8.3-to-1. Central chain-driven camshaft. Bore, 88.9 mm, stroke 88.4 mm; capacity 4389 cc. Power (SAE): 115 bhp (86 kW) at 4000 rpm; torque 205 lb ft (283 Nm) at 2400 rpm.

Transmission: Rear-wheel drive; Hydra-Matic three-speed automatic transmission standard. Top gear mph at 1000 rpm: 31.3.

Suspension: Front, independent, wishbones and coil springs; telescopic dampers. Anti-roll bar. Rear, live axle on longitudinal links, with upper links to diff. Coil springs and telescopic dampers. Anti-roll bar optional.

Steering: Recirculating ball, power assisted.

Brakes: Vented discs front, drums rear, servo-assisted.

Tyres: 195/75 SR 14.

Dimensions: Length 5090 mm (220.4 in), width 1825 mm (71.8 in), height 1380 mm (54.3 in), wheelbase 2745 mm (108.1 in).

Unladen weight: 1515 kg (3340 lb).

Performance (est.): Maximum speed, 98 mph. Fuel consumption, 19 mpg (at constant 75 mph).

Features: Four rectangular headlamps identify the current model. Well-equipped, and interior decor substantially revised and improved for 1983. California gets 5-litre V8 option instead of 4.4-litre.

CHRYSLER (USA)   Cordoba

Identity: Two-door coupé body; also available is the cabriolet, designed to look like a convertible—complete with the drawback of blind rear quarters!—but is actually a fixed head. Choice of 6-cylinder 3.7-litre engine (detailed below) or 5.2-litre V8.

Engine: Front-mounted six-cylinder with pushrod ohv. Cast iron head and block. Unleaded fuel (leaded fuel versions available). Bore, 86.4 mm, stroke 104.6 mm; capacity 3,680 cc. Power (SAE): 90 bhp (67 kW) at 3,600 rpm; torque 160 lb ft (221 Nm) at 1600 rpm.

Transmission: Rear-wheel drive; TorqueFlite automatic three-speed transmission. Top gear mph at 1000 rpm: 26.0.

Suspension: Front, independent, transverse unequal length arms and transverse torsion bars. Telescopic dampers. Anti-roll bar optional. Rear, live axle on semi-elliptic leaf springs. Telescopic dampers. Anti-roll bar optional.

Steering: Recirculating ball, power assisted.

Brakes: Vented discs front, drums rear, servo-assisted.

Tyres: 195/75 R 15.

Dimensions: Length 5337 mm (210.1 in), width 1847 mm (72.7 in), height 1351 mm (53.2 in), wheelbase 2863 mm (112.7 in).

Unladen weight: 1570 kg (3460 lb).

Performance (est.): Maximum speed, 94 mph. Fuel consumption, 18 mpg (overall).

Features: Cloth and vinyl seats; halogen headlamps. Choice of seat styles. Cabriolet roof package (simulated convertible) is also an option. Less fully equipped version is Cordoba LS.

CHRYSLER (USA) LeBaron convertible

Identity: Launched spring 1982, the LeBaron is offered as two- or four-door saloon, estate car, or two-door convertible. Choice of 2.2- or 2.6-litre, with four cylinders. Engine mounted transversely. Identity name of convertible is Medallion.

Engine: Front-mounted four-cylinder with alloy head and single ohc, belt-driven. Unleaded fuel. Compression 8.2-to-1. Bore, 91.1 mm, stroke 98 mm; capacity 2555 cc. Power (SAE): 92 bhp (68.5 kW) at 4,500 rpm; torque 132 lb ft (179 Nm) at 2,500 rpm.

Transmission: Front-wheel drive: five-speed manual gearbox (on two-door model); automatic three-speed transmission optional. Top gear mph at 1,000 rpm: 24.9.

Suspension: Front, independent, MacPherson struts and coil springs; telescopic dampers. Anti-roll bar. Rear, dead beam axle on trailing links and Panhard rod; coil springs and telescopic dampers. Anti-roll bar.

Steering: Rack and pinion; power assistance optional.

Brakes: Vented discs front, drums rear, servo-assisted.

Tyres: 185/70 R 14.

Dimensions: Length 4564 mm (180 in), width 1740 mm (68.5 in), height 1335 mm (52.6 in), wheelbase 2540 mm (100 in).

Unladen weight: 1155 kg (2546 lb).

Performance (est.): Maximum speed, 103 mph. Fuel consumption, 19 mpg (overall).

Features: Stylish convertible, with full folding hood and tonneau cover. Hardtop version also available. Four oblong headlamps in deep recesses, and sloping radiator grille.

CITROEN (F)

Identity: New mid-range generation of Citroens launched Paris 1982 with futuristic look and significant development in form of plastic materials for bonnet, rear hatch and some other components. New engines with water cooling and capacity of 1,360 or 1580 cc (detailed below). Engine mounting transverse and leaning rearward.

Engine: Front-mounted four-cylinder inclined rearwards at angle of 30 deg (72 deg for 1360 unit). Cylinders in-line, and belt-driven ohc. Head and block of alloy, cast iron liners. Bore, 83 mm, stroke 73 mm; capacity 1580 cc. Power, 90 bhp (67 kW) at 6000 rpm; torque 94 lb ft (130 Nm) at 3500 rpm.

Transmission: Front-wheel drive; manual five-speed gearbox in-line with engine. Top gear mph at 1000 rpm: 21.1.

Suspension: Front, independent, wishbones and Citroen hydropneumatic units. Anti-roll bar. Rear, independent, trailing arms and Citroen hydropneumatic units. Automatic self-levelling. Anti-roll bar.

Steering: Rack and pinion.

Brakes: Discs front and rear, servo-assisted.

Tyres: 170/65 R 365 Michelin TRX.

Dimensions: Length 4230 mm (166.5 in), width 1650 mm (65 in), height 1361 mm (53.6 in), wheelbase 2655 mm (104.5 in).

Unladen weight: 940 kg (2072 lb).

Performance (Works): Maximum speed, 109 mph. 0 to 60 mph, 11.5 sec. Fuel consumption, 38.2 mpg (at constant 75 mph).

Features: Four door body with hatchback tail which lifts up taking rear shelf with it on cords. Fascinating, pace-setting design.

CITROEN (F)   2CV 6 Charleston

Identity: First launched as a special version of the little 2CV which dates back to 1948, the Charleston entered the range as a production option. Distinctive paint stripes continue the upper curvature of the windows down to the doors.

Engine: Front-mounted two-cylinder with air-cooling and horizontally opposed layout. Compression 8.5-to-1. Bore, 74 mm, stroke 70 mm; capacity 602 cc. Power, 28.5 bhp (21.5 kW) at 5750 rpm; torque 28 lb ft (39 Nm) at 3,500 rpm.

Transmission: Front-wheel drive; four-speed gear change with push-pull action, mounted on facia. All gears indirect. Top gear mph at 1000 rpm: 12.7.

Suspension: Front, independent, leading arms and coil springs; telescopic dampers. Very soft springing. Rear, independent, leading arms and coil springs; telescopic dampers.

Steering: Rack and pinion.

Brakes: Discs front, drums rear.

Tyres: 125-15 Michelin X, 4J.

Dimensions: Length 3830 mm (150 in), width 1480 mm (58 in), height 1600 mm (63 in), wheelbase 2400 mm (95 in).

Unladen weight: 585 kg (1289 lb).

Performance: Maximum speed, 69 mph. 0 to 60 mph, 32.7 sec. Fuel consumption, 52 mpg (at constant 56 mph).

Features: Cheerful utility car with cheekily distinctive appearance and functional space; remarkable economy, and performance fair once speed has been built up. Roll-back sunroof.

CITROEN (F)　　CX 2500 D Safari Reflex

Identity: Estate version of the big Citroen, with two-level roof line, and huge carrying capacity. Available also as the Familiale, with same body but three rows of seats, to accommodate seven adults, still with quite a lot of rear luggage space.

Engine: Front-mounted transverse four-cylinder with alloy head and 22.3-to-1 compression for diesel operation. Bore, 93 mm, stroke 92 mm; capacity 2500 cc. Power, 75 bhp (56 kW) at 4250 rpm; torque 111 lb ft (153 Nm) at 2000 rpm.

Transmission: Front-wheel drive; five-speed manual transmission (no automatic option for diesel versions). Top gear mph at 1000 rpm: 22.1.

Suspension: Front, independent, double transverse arms, Hydropneumatic system with dampers incorporated in springs. Anti-roll bar. Rear, independent, trailing arms, Hydropneumatic system with dampers incorporated in springs. Anti-roll bar. Pressurised self-levelling, powered by engine-driven pump.

Steering: Rack and pinion, VariPower system giving speed-sensitive response.

Brakes: Ventilated discs front and rear, power operated off central hydraulic system.

Tyres: 185 SR 14.

Dimensions: Length 4952 mm (195 in), width 1734 mm (68 in), height 1465 mm (57.6 in), wheelbase 3095 mm (122 in).

Unladen weight: 1458 kg (3213 lb).

Performance: Maximum speed, 94 mph. 0 to 60 mph, 17.2 sec. Fuel consumption, 32.1 mpg (at constant 75 mph).

Features: Remarkable load-carrying ability, and an unrivalled combination of space, speed and economy; slightly bulky in congested areas, but really at home in fast cruising.

Identity: Latest version of medium-range Citroen with horizontally opposed air-cooled engine and self-levelling Hydropneumatic suspension. Introduced September 1982 with slightly lower gear ratio to give extra performance in fifth. Spoilers front and rear.

Engine: Front-mounted four-cylinder with horizontally-opposed layout for all-alloy unit. Toothed belt camshaft drive, ohc each head. Bore, 79.4 mm, stroke 65.6 mm; capacity 1299 cc. Power, 65 bhp (48.5 kW) at 5,500 rpm; torque 72 lb ft (100 Nm) at 3500 rpm.

Transmission: Front-wheel drive; five-speed gearbox standard (no automatic option). Spiral bevel final drive. Top gear mph at 1,000 rpm: 17.7.

Suspension: Front, independent, double wishbones and Hydropneumatic self-levelling units; anti-roll bar. Rear, independent, trailing arms and Hydropneumatic self-levelling units; anti-roll bar.

Steering: Rack and pinion.

Brakes: Discs front and rear, servo-assisted.

Tyres: 145 SR 15.

Dimensions: Length 4120 mm (162 in), width 1608 mm (63.3 in), height 1349 mm (53 in), wheelbase 2550 mm (100.4 in).

Unladen weight: 992 kg (2184 lb).

Performance: Maximum speed, 95 mph (fourth and fifth). 0 to 60 mph, 14.9 sec. Fuel consumption, 31.7 mpg (at constant 75 mph).

Features: Extremely comfortable ride and seats; good interior space for size of car. Provision for rear bench seat to fold down, and detachable rear shelf in hatchback five-door body.

CITROEN (F)   Visa GT

Identity: New model introduced Paris 1982, to replace Visa II Super X. Alterations to suspension to give better roadholding, and more powerful 1360 cc engine provides lively performance and faster cruising.

Engine: Front-mounted four-cylinder with chain-driven single ohc; alloy head and block, with wet cylinder liners. Compression ratio 9.3-to-1. Transverse mounting. Bore, 75 mm, stroke 77 mm; capacity 1360 cc. Power, 80 bhp (57 kW) at 5800 rpm; torque 79 lb ft (109 Nm) at 2800 rpm.

Transmission: Front-wheel drive; five-speed manual gearbox standard (no automatic option). Final drive ratio 3.87-to-1. Top gear mph at 1000 rpm: 17.8.

Suspension: Front, independent, MacPherson struts; coil springs and telescopic dampers. Anti-roll bar. Rear, independent, trailing arms; coil springs and telescopic dampers. Anti-roll bar.

Steering: Rack and pinion.

Brakes: Discs front, drums rear, servo-assisted.

Tyres: 160/65 R 340 TRX.

Dimensions: Length 3721 mm (146.5 in), width 1537 mm (60.5 in), height 1417 mm (55.8 in), wheelbase 2419 mm (95.3 in).

Unladen weight: 800 kg (1764 lb).

Performance (Works): Maximum speed, 104 mph. 0 to 60 mph, 10.9 sec. Fuel consumption, 38.2 mpg (at constant 75 mph).

Features: Alloy wheels and Michelin TRX tyres standard. Redesigned seats; split rear seat, independently folding for extra stowage space. GT badge on bonnet, front air dam, and rear spoiler.

COLT (J) (MITSUBISHI)

1400 GLX Hatchback Turbo

Identity: High performance version of three-door 1400 Hatchback with turbocharged engine and many changes to suit the car to much higher speeds.

Engine: Front-mounted transverse four-cylinder with cylinders in-line, overhead camshaft, and turbocharger between carburettor and engine. Bore, 74 mm, stroke 82 mm; capacity 1410 cc. Power, 104 bhp (78 kW) at 5,500 rpm; torque 114 lb ft (158 Nm) at 3,500 rpm.

Transmission: Front-wheel drive; four-speed gearbox with additional lever alongside to change transmission range giving total choice of eight forward ratios. Top gear mph at 1,000 rpm: 17.5/22.7.

Suspension: Front, independent, MacPherson struts, telescopic dampers; anti-roll bar. Rear, independent, trailing arms and coil springs, telescopic dampers; anti-roll bar.

Steering: Rack and pinion.

Brakes: Ventilated discs front, drums rear, servo-assisted.

Tyres: 175/70 HR 13.

Dimensions: Length 3790 mm (149 in), width 1585 mm (62.4 in), height 1345 mm (53 in), wheelbase 2300 mm (90.6 in).

Unladen weight: 853 kg (1879 lb).

Performance: Maximum speed, 105 mph. 0 to 60 mph, 9.9 sec. Fuel consumption, 32.1 mpg (at constant 75 mph).

Features: Impressive acceleration right through to 100 mph, but abrupt power limit imposed by devices to prevent excess turbo boost limit top speed. Good fast cruising, though rather noisy. Car well adapted to cope with the extra performance.

61

COLT (J)   Galant 2000 Estate Car

Identity: Spacious dual-purpose vehicle, evolved from Galant Saloon, with four doors and longer flat load space with spare wheel mounted vertically on left. Good general purpose vehicle. Choice of 1600, 1800 or 2-litre engine (detailed below).

Engine: Front-mounted four-cylinder with alloy head, single chain-driven ohc, and twin counter-rotating balance shafts for smoothness. Bore, 85 mm, stroke 88 mm; capacity 1997 cc. Power, 109 bhp (81 kW) at 5500 rpm; torque 119 lb ft (164 Nm) at 3500 rpm.

Transmission: Rear-wheel drive; choice of four- or five-speed manual gearbox, or three-speed automatic. Anti-roll bar. Top gear mph at 1,000 rpm: 21.1.

Suspension: Front, independent, MacPherson struts. Coil springs and telescopic dampers. Rear, independent, semi-trailing arms and coil springs. Telescopic dampers.

Steering: Recirculating ball.

Brakes: Discs front and rear, servo-assisted.

Tyres: 185/70 HR 14.

Dimensions: Length 4465 mm (175.8 in), width 1655 mm (65.2 in), height 1385 mm (54.5 in), wheelbase 2530 mm (99.6 in).

Unladen weight: 1085 kg (2392 lb).

Performance: Maximum speed, 103 mph. 0 to 60 mph, 11.9 sec. Fuel consumption, 28.8 mpg (at constant 75 mph).

Features: Well-equipped, and good combination of generous roominess in a vehicle that is still pleasantly compact and easy to drive. Performs quite well and suspension copes with heavy loads without problems.

Identity: First of the rapidly growing line of turbocharged cars from Colt (Mitsubishi). Straightforward design, but an exciting and very manageable performance car. Turbo 2000 lettering in reverse on front, spoilers front and rear, and (usually) large Hella foglamps are identifying features.

Engine: Front-mounted four-cylinder with aluminium head on cast iron block, and single belt-driven ohc. Mitsubishi-Bosch electronic injection, and Mitsubishi turbocharger. Bore, 85 mm, stroke 88 mm; capacity 1997 cc. Power, 168 bhp (125 kW) at 5,500 rpm; torque 181 lb ft (250 Nm) at 3,500 rpm.

Transmission: Rear-wheel drive; five-speed gearbox; hypoid bevel final drive, with ratio 3.55-to-1. Top gear mph at 1000 rpm: 23.2.

Suspension: Front, independent, MacPherson struts; coil springs and telescopic gas-filled dampers. Anti-roll bar. Rear, live axle on four trailing links (two semi-trailing for lateral location); coil springs and telescopic gas-filled dampers.

Steering: Recirculating ball.

Brakes: Vented discs front, solid discs rear, servo-assisted.

Tyres: 175/70 HR 14.

Dimensions: Length 4225 mm (166 in), width 1620 mm (64 in), height 1385 mm (54.5 in), wheelbase 2440 mm (96 in).

Unladen weight: 1061 kg (2336 lb).

Performance: Maximum speed, 127 mph. 0 to 60 mph, 8.6 sec. Fuel consumption, 28.8 mpg (at constant 75 mph).

Features: Eager performance, high cruising speed, and unexpectedly good (in view of simple layout) roadholding and handling; ride rather firm. Snug seats and good instrument layout.

COLT (J) (MITSUBISHI)   Starion 2000 Turbo

Identity: Striking four-seater two-door coupé with opening rear window. Pop-up headlamps. Ingenious seat belt arrangement, mounted in doors. Air scoop on bonnet. Energy absorbing bumpers, integral with body at front.

Engine: Front-mounted single ohc four-cylinder with cylinders in-line in cast iron block. Electronic fuel injection and Mitsubishi turbocharger. Bore, 85 mm, stroke 88 mm; capacity 1997 cc. Power, 168 bhp (125 kw) at 5,500 rpm; torque 181 lb ft (250 Nm) at 3,500 rpm.

Transmission: Rear-wheel drive; five-speed gearbox; limited slip final drive. S.d.p. clutch with hydraulic control. Top gear mph at 1,000 rpm: 24.4.

Suspension: Front, independent, MacPherson struts, telescopic dampers, anti-roll bar. Rear, independent, MacPherson struts and lower links; coil springs and telescopic dampers. Anti-roll bar.

Steering: Recirculating ball with power assistance.

Brakes: Disc front and rear, servo-assisted.

Tyres: 205/70 VR 14.

Dimensions: Length 4425 mm (174 in), width 1705 mm (67 in), height 1315 mm (52 in), wheelbase 2435 mm (96 in).

Unladen weight: 1225 kg (2700 lb).

Performance: Maximum speed, 133 mph. 0 to 60 mph, 7.5 sec. Fuel consumption, 29.9 mpg (at constant 75 mph).

Features: Good performance, very safe handling and excellent brakes. Rear seats fold for extra luggage space, but boot space severely limited. Impressive GT car. Alloy wheels standard.

DAIHATSU (J)   Charade XTE

Identity: Small five-door hatchback with fascinating novelty of design, chief feature being the use of a three-cylinder engine. Potentially very economical. One of the smallest cars to have a five-speed gearbox.

Engine: Front-mounted three-cylinder with alloy head, and ohc with toothed belt drive. Compression 9.0-to-1. Contact breaker. Bore, 76 mm, stroke 73 mm; capacity 993 cc. Power, 50 bhp (37 kW) at 5500 rpm; torque 53.5 lb ft (74 Nm) at 3000 rpm.

Transmission: Front-wheel drive; five-speed manual gearbox. Helical spur final drive, ratio 4.27-to-1. Top gear mph at 1,000 rpm: 18.5.

Suspension: Front, independent, MacPherson struts and coil springs; telescopic dampers. Rear, dead beam axle on trailing arms and Panhard rod. Telescopic dampers; coil springs.

Steering: Rack and pinion.

Brakes: Discs front, drums rear, servo-assisted.

Tyres: 155 SR 12.

Dimensions: Length 3485 mm (137 in), width 1510 mm (59.4 in), height 1345 mm (53 in), wheelbase 2300 mm (90.6 in).

Unladen weight: 688 kg (1517 lb).

Performance: Maximum speed, 83 mph (fourth). 0 to 60 mph, 16.1 sec. Fuel consumption, 32.2 mpg (at constant 75 mph).

Features: Quite well equipped for such a small and relatively inexpensive car, and quite nippy with good cruising ability, but very noisy. Handling not very reassuring.

DAIHATSU (J)   Charmant 1600LE

Identity: Comparatively recent addition to British market, though the make is long-established on other markets. Conventional design for three-box saloon body with four doors and engine at front with in-line layout and drive to rear wheels. Main merit is value for money.

Engine: Front-mounted four-cylinder with single ohc driven by chain. Alloy head on cast iron block. Breakerless ignition. Bore, 85 mm, stroke 70 mm; capacity 1588 cc. Power, 74 bhp (55 kW) at 5400 rpm; torque 87 lb ft (120 Nm) at 3,600 rpm.

Transmission: Rear-wheel drive; five-speed gearbox standard; three-speed automatic optional. Hypoid bevel final drive, ratio 3.91-to-1. Top gear mph at 1000 rpm: 19.3.

Suspension: Front, independent, MacPherson struts; coil springs and telescopic dampers. Anti-roll bar. Rear, live axle on trailing links and Panhard rod. Coil springs and telescopic dampers.

Steering: Recirculating ball.

Brakes: Discs front, drums rear, servo-assisted.

Tyres: 175/70 SR 13.

Dimensions: Length 4150 mm (163 in), width 1625 mm (64 in), height 1379 mm (54.3 in), wheelbase 2400 mm (94.5 in).

Unladen weight: 950 kg (2094 lb).

Performance; Maximum speed, 94 mph. 0 to 60 mph, 13.2 sec. Fuel consumption, 31.1 mpg (at constant 75 mph).

Features: Quite pleasantly high-geared and quiet, roomy car with good equipment for price range. Spoilt by rather indifferent suspension and vague steering.

DAIMLER (GB)   DS 420 Limousine

Identity: Originally introduced 1968, but still prime choice for embassies, state processional transport and so on. Bodies originally built by Vanden Plas, but since transferred to the Jaguar works at Coventry.

Engine: Front-mounted six-cylinder with twin ohc, chain-driven. Twin SU carbs. Compression only 7.5-to-1. Bore, 92.1 mm, stroke 106 mm; capacity 4235 cc. Power, 165 bhp (123 kW) at 4250 rpm; torque 224 lb ft (309 Nm) at 3000 rpm.

Transmission: Rear-wheel drive; Borg-Warner automatic three-speed transmission. Top gear mph at 1000 rpm: 21.6.

Suspension: Front, independent, wishbones and coil springs; telescopic dampers. Anti-roll bar. Rear, independent, transverse arms, twin coil springs each side; telescopic dampers.

Steering: Recirculating ball, power assisted.

Brakes: Discs front and (inboard) rear, servo-assisted.

Tyres: 205/70 HR 15.

Dimensions: Length 5740 mm (226 in), width 1995 mm (78.5 in), height 1620 mm (63.8 in), wheelbase 3580 mm (141 in).

Unladen weight: 2140 kg (4718 lb).

Performance (Works): Maximum speed, 110 mph. 0 to 50 mph, 9.2 sec. Fuel consumption, 15.5 mpg (at constant 75 mph).

Features: Magnificently finished, with upholstery in West of England cloth, polished walnut door trim and facia, and superbly comfortable—but mainly for state occasions.

DAIMLER (GB)

Double-Six HE

Identity: Familiar lines of the Jaguar XJ lwb saloon with Daimler traditional fluted radiator grille and luxury fittings, and in the much more acceptable High Efficiency form with May combustion chambers, as introduced mid-1981.

Engine: Front-mounted V12-cylinder with single ohc each bank, Lucas injection and all-alloy construction. Compression 12.5-to-1. Bore, 90 mm. stroke 70 mm; capacity 5345 cc. Power, 299 bhp (223 kW) at 5500 rpm; torque 318 lb ft (440 Nm) at 3000 rpm.

Transmission: Rear-wheel drive; GM Turbo Hydra-Matic 400 automatic transmission; no manual version. Top gear mph at 1000 rpm: 26.9.

Suspension: Front, independent, wishbones and coil springs; anti-dive geometry; telescopic dampers. Anti-roll bar. Rear, independent, radius arms, transverse lower links, and twin coil springs and telescopic dampers each side.

Steering: Rack and pinion, power assisted.

Brakes: Discs front (vented) and rear, servo-assisted.

Tyres: 215/70 VR 15 Dunlop D7.

Dimensions: Length 4951 mm (195 in), width 1770 mm (70 in), height 1374 mm (54 in), wheelbase 2865 mm (113 in).

Unladen weight: 1914 kg (4219 lb).

Performance: Maximum speed, 150 mph. 0 to 60 mph, 8.1 sec. Fuel consumption, 21.5 mpg (at constant 75 mph).

Features: Magnificent comfort, and a combination of speed, refinement, handling and quietness that few—if any—cars in the world can match. Very fully equipped.

DATSUN (J)   **Cherry**

Identity: Re-bodied range of small cars introduced with choice of six models on British market September 1982. Much improved appearance and more aerodynamic shape. E-Series engines developed for economy. Three- or five-door hatchback.

Engine: Front-mounted four-cylinder with overhead camshaft. Transverse installation; gearbox and final drive in line. Compression 9.0-to-1. Bore, 76 mm, stroke 70 mm; capacity 1270 cc. Power, 60 bhp (45 kW) at 5600 rpm; torque 74 lb ft (102 Nm) at 3600 rpm.

Transmission: Front-wheel drive; five-speed manual gearbox standard except on cheapest version—four-speed (automatic available only with 1.5-litre engine). Final drive ratio 3.9-to-1. Top gear mph at 1000 rpm: 23.1.

Suspension: Front, independent, MacPherson struts; coil springs and telescopic dampers. Anti-roll bar. Rear, independent, semi-trailing arms; coil springs and telescopic dampers.

Steering: Rack and pinion.

Brakes: Discs front, drums rear, servo-assisted.

Tyres: 155 SR 13.

Dimensions: Length 3960 mm (155.9 in), width 1621 mm (63.8 in), height 1384 mm (54.5 in), wheelbase 2416 mm (95.1 in).

Unladen weight: 805 kg (1775 lb).

Performance (Works): Maximum speed, 96 mph. 0 to 60 mph, 14.4 sec. Fuel consumption, 32.8 mpg (at constant 75 mph).

Features: Cloth seats and tinted glass standard. Tilt-adjustable steering column. Rear wash/wipe. Door mirrors with internal adjustment on GL, plus interior releases for fuel flap and tailgate.

DATSUN (J)   Sunny 1.5DX

Identity: Completely new version of popular small family car from Datsun with more 'European' styling, reduced weight, and availability of larger engine. Produced in three body styles—saloon, coupé, or estate car—and with 1.3 or (detailed below) 1.5 engines. 1.3 DX has two doors, as does the Coupé.

Engine: Front-mounted transverse four-cylinder with single belt-driven ohc. Alloy head on cast iron block. Compression 9.8-to-1. Bore, 76 mm, stroke 82 mm; capacity 1488 cc. Power, 75 bhp (56 kW) at 5000 rpm; torque 91 lb ft (125 Nm) at 2800 rpm.

Transmission: Front-wheel drive; five-speed gearbox standard, and helical spur final drive. Three-speed automatic transmission available for 1.5 saloon and estate (extra). Top gear mph at 1000 rpm: 25.3.

Suspension: Front, independent, MacPherson struts; coil springs and telescopic dampers. Anti-roll bar. Rear, independent, trailing arms; coil springs and telescopic dampers.

Steering: Rack and pinion.

Brakes: Discs front, drums rear, servo-assisted.

Tyres: 155 SR 13.

Dimensions: Length 4050 mm (159.4 in), width 1620 mm (64 in), height 1385 mm (54.5 in), wheelbase 2400 mm (94.5 in).

Unladen weight: 829 kg (1828 lb).

Performance: Maximum speed, 95 mph (fourth). 0 to 60 mph, 11.0 sec. Fuel consumption, 42.8 mpg (at constant 75 mph).

Features: High gearing for size of car and engine contributes to good economy, and performance is also quite lively. Typical Japanese interior—ultra-neat.

DATSUN (J)   Stanza

Identity: Datsun's mid-range front-drive car, saloon and hatchback, launched in mid-1981. Choice of three, four or five doors.

Engine: Front-mounted four-cylinder in-line, transverse-mounted, with chain-driven overhead camshaft, 1600 (data follows) or 1800. Bore, 78 mm, stroke 83.6 mm; capacity 1598 cc. Power, 81 bhp (60 kW) at 5200 rpm; torque 96 lb ft. (133 Nm) at 5200 rpm.

Transmission: Front-wheel drive; four-speed gearbox on basic saloon, five-speed on others; automatic three-speed option for five-door SGL. Top gear mph at 1000 rpm: 25.3.

Suspension: Front, independent, MacPherson struts, telescopic dampers; no anti-roll bar. Rear, independent, MacPherson struts with parallel links and radius rods; telescopic dampers, no anti-roll bar.

Steering: Rack and pinion; power assistance on SGL.

Brakes: Discs front, drums rear, servo-assisted.

Tyres: 165 SR 13.

Dimensions: Length 4280 mm (168.5 in), width 1665 mm (66 in), height 1385 mm (55 in), wheelbase 2470 mm (97 in).

Unladen weight: 870 kg (1916 lb).

Performance: Maximum speed, 96 mph. 0 to 60 mph, 12.0 sec. Fuel consumption, 37.7 mpg (at constant 75 mph).

Features: Rather severe understeer, but good space, practical layout, and advantage of split rear seat on hatchback. 1800 engine fitted only with automatic transmission in UK. All other models 1600.

DATSUN (J)

Identity: Sporting 2+2 available with individual Targa top. Conventional design, good performance, but less appeal now than when first introduced in 1969.

Engine: Front-mounted six-cylinder with in-line construction and alloy head. Available also with turbocharger. Electronic ignition. Bore, 86 mm, stroke 79 mm; capacity 2753 cc. Power, 146 bhp (109 kW) at 5250 rpm; torque 155 lb ft (214 Nm) at 4500 rpm.

Transmission: Rear-wheel drive; five-speed gearbox standard. Final drive ratio 3.7-to-1. Automatic three-speed transmission available. Top gear mph at 1000 rpm: 22.7.

Suspension: Front, independent, MacPherson struts and coil springs; telescopic dampers. Anti-roll bar. Rear, independent, semi-trailing arms and coil springs; telescopic dampers. Anti-roll bar.

Steering: Rack and pinion; power assistance optional.

Brakes: Discs front, and rear, servo-assisted.

Tyres: 195/70 HR 14.

Dimensions: Length 4539 mm (179 in), width 1690 mm (66.5 in), height 1300 mm (51.2 in), wheelbase 2520 mm (99.2 in).

Unladen weight: 1230 kg (2711 lb).

Performance (Automatic): Maximum speed, 111 mph. 0 to 60 mph, 11.3 sec. Fuel consumption, 27.7 mpg (at constant 75 mph).

Features: Comprehensive instrumentation and good equipment. Comfortable seats, but limited rear leg room. Neat finish.

Identity: Big-bodied cross-country vehicle available with estate car two- or four-door body. Divided tailgate, top-hinged window and let-down panel. Large ground clearance and good cross-country performance. Choice of petrol or diesel engines.

Engine: Front-mounted six-cylinder with pushrod ohv, Hitachi carb. Bore, 85.7 mm, stroke 114.3 mm; capacity 3956 cc. Power, 135 bhp (101 kW) at 3600 rpm; torque 213 lb ft (294 Nm) at 2000 rpm.

Transmission: Four-wheel drive; four-speed manual gearbox. Normal drive to rear wheels; fwd selectable in addition, plus low ratio transfer. Top gear mph at 1000 rpm: 19.1.

Suspension: Front, live axle on semi-elliptic leaf springs; telescopic dampers. Anti-roll bar. Rear, live axle, on semi-elliptic leaf springs; telescopic dampers. Anti-roll bar.

Steering: Recirculating ball, power assisted.

Brakes: Vented discs front, drums rear, servo-assisted.

Tyres: 205 R 16.

Dimensions (Estate car): Length 4690 mm (184.6 in), width 1690 mm (66.5 in), height 1835 mm (72.2 in), wheelbase 2970 mm (117 in).

Unladen weight: 1675 kg (3693 lb).

Performance (Works): Maximum speed, 87 mph. Fuel consumption, 16.4 mpg (at constant 75 mph).

Features: Generous interior accommodation. Lwb has rear seat split at one third width. Separate range change selector lever. Large grab handle on facia in front of passenger.

DE TOMASO (I)   Pantera GTS

Identity: Exciting high performance coupé with mid-engined layout and using an almost standard Ford V8 unit. Originally launched New York, 1970; little changed since.

Engine: Mid-mounted V8-cylinder with pushrod ohv. Autolite carburettor. Compression 11.0-to-1. Cylinders in 90 deg V. Bore, 101.6 mm, stroke 89 mm; capacity 5769 cc. Power, 266 bhp (198.5 kW) at 5600 rpm; torque 319 lb ft (441 Nm) at 3500 rpm.

Transmission: Rear-wheel drive; ZF five-speed gearbox in transaxle at rear of engine; no automatic version. Final drive ratio 4.22-to-1. Limited slip diff. Top gear mph at 1000 rpm: 26.3.

Suspension: Front, independent, wishbones and coil spring-damper units. Anti-roll bar. Rear, independent, wishbones and coil spring-damper units. Anti-roll bar.

Steering: Rack and pinion.

Brakes: Vented discs front, and rear, servo-assisted.

Tyres: 185/70 HR 15.

Dimensions: Length 4270 mm (168 in), width 1830 mm (72 in), height 110 mm (43.3 in), wheelbase 2515 mm (99 in).

Unladen weight: 1420 kg (3130 lb).

Performance: Maximum speed, 159 mph. 0 to 60 mph, 6.2 sec. Fuel consumption, 15.8 mpg (at constant 75 mph).

Features: Very well-balanced cornering and good, taut ride. Very noisy, but in keeping with spectacular performance. Brakes not as good as specification implies, rather lacking response when cold. Poor handbrake. Impressive interior appearance.

Identity: Spacious four-door saloon introduced for 1983 model year, similar to previous 400 model. Oblong headlamps in deep recesses, and slatted grille, with additional intake slot in bumper. Four-cylinder transverse engine and front drive; choice of 2.2- or 2.6-litre. Details below are for 2.6.

Engine: Front-mounted four-cylinder with belt-driven ohc. Alloy head. Unleaded fuel, compression ratio 8.2-to-1. Bore, 91.1 mm, stroke 98 mm; capacity 2556 cc. Power (SAE): 93 bhp (69 kW) at 4500 rpm; torque 132 lb ft (179 Nm) at 2500 rpm.

Transmission: Front-wheel drive; three-speed automatic transmission standard, with column-mounted selector. Manual option for 2.2-litre only. Top gear mph at 1000 rpm: 23.1.

Suspension: Front, independent, MacPherson struts; coil springs and telescopic dampers. Anti-roll bar. Rear, dead beam axle on trailing arms, with Panhard rod; coil springs and telescopic dampers. Anti-roll bar.

Steering: Rack and pinion, power assisted.

Brakes: Discs front, drums rear, servo-assisted.

Tyres: 185/70 R 14.

Dimensions: Length 4754 mm (187.2 in), width 1734 mm (68.3 in), height 1346 mm (52.9 in), wheelbase 2618 mm (103.1 in).

Unladen weight: 1203 kg (2646 lb).

Performance (est.): Maximum speed, 100 mph. Fuel consumption, 20 mpg (overall).

Features: Well-equipped, with such details as map lamp, under-bonnet lamp, and fuel flap remote release. Wide range of options.

EXCALIBUR (USA)   Series IV Phaeton

Identity: Nostalgic design based on historic Mercedes-Benz 540K, with two-door open bodywork and available as two-door roadster or as six-seater tourer with power adjustment for seats, and power-operated hood.

Engine: Front-mounted GM V8-cylinder with 8.6-to-1 compression, and Rochester carburettor, fully de-toxed with stainless steel exhaust. Bore 94.9 mm, stroke 88.4 mm; capacity 4998 cc. Power, 155 bhp (116 kW) at 4,000 rpm; torque 225 lb ft (311 Nm) at 2400 rpm.

Transmission: Rear-wheel drive; three-speed Hydramatic 400 automatic transmission, no manual version available. Top gear mph at 1000 rpm: 29.8.

Suspension: Front, independent, wishbones and coil springs; anti-roll bar. Telescopic dampers. Rear, independent, transverse leaf spring, angular strut rods, radius arms, half shafts and self-levelling telescopic dampers.

Steering: Varying ratio recirculating ball; power assisted.

Brakes: Discs front and rear, servo-assisted.

Tyres: 235 R 75–15.

Dimensions: Length 5258 mm (207 in), width 1905 mm (75 in), height 1499 mm (59 in), wheelbase 3175 mm (125 in).

Unladen weight: 2043 kg (4500 lb).

Performance (Works): Maximum speed, 112 mph.

Features: Lavishly equipped, with leather upholstery, teak facia, cruise control, electric window lifts, and air conditioning.

FERRARI (I)

308 GTBi

Identity: Two-seater with removable targa top (GTSi), or fixed head (GTBi), mechanically similar to the Dino 308 GT 4. Mid-engined layout, and engine with fuel injection since autumn 1980.

Engine: Mid-mounted V8-cylinder with twin ohc each bank of cylinders. Alloy construction and Bosch K-Jetronic injection. Bore, 81 mm, stroke 71 mm; capacity 2927 cc. Power, 211 bhp (157.5 kW) at 6600 rpm; torque 175.8 lb ft (243 Nm) at 4600 rpm.

Transmission: Rear-wheel drive; five-speed manual gearbox (no automatic version available). Top gear mph at 1000 rpm: 22.1.

Suspension: Front, independent, wishbones and coil springs; telescopic dampers. Anti-roll bar. Rear, independent, wishbones and coil springs; telescopic dampers. Anti-roll bar.

Steering: Rack and pinion.

Brakes: Discs front (vented) and rear, servo-assisted.

Tyres: 205/55 VR 16 (front), 225/55 VR 16 (rear).

Dimensions: Length 4230 mm (166.5 in), width 1720 mm (68 in), height 1120 mm (44 in), wheelbase 2340 mm (92 in).

Unladen weight: 1340 kg (2952 lb).

Performance (Works): Maximum speed, 149 mph. Fuel consumption, 22.6 mpg (at constant 75 mph).

Features: Least expensive of the fabulous Ferrari range, offering very impressive performance, superb handling, and not quite such formidable running costs and fuel consumption as dearer models. Restricted accommodation—but worth travelling light!

Identity: 2 + 2 high performance GT with mid-engined layout and new body developed by Pininfarina, launched Geneva 1980. Look for slatted air intakes ahead of rear wheels.

Engine: Mid-mounted V8-cylinder with twin ohc each bank, and alloy heads and block. Compression 8.8-to-1. Bore, 81 mm, stroke 71 mm; capacity 2927 cc. Power, 211 bhp (157.5 kW) at 6600 rpm; torque 176 lb ft (243 Nm) at 4600 rpm.

Transmission: Rear-wheel drive; five-speed manual gearbox with short-travel change. No automatic option. Top gear mph at 1000 rpm: 20.0.

Suspension: Front, independent, coil springs and wishbones; telescopic dampers. Anti-roll bar. Rear, independent, coil springs and wishbones; telescopic dampers. Anti-roll bar.

Steering: Rack and pinion.

Brakes: Vented discs front and rear, servo-assisted.

Tyres: 240/55 VR 390.

Dimensions: Length 4572 mm (180 in), width 1791 mm (70.5 in), height 1250 mm (49.2 in), wheelbase 2550 mm (100.4 in).

Unladen weight: 1504 kg (3316 lb).

Performance (Works): Maximum speed, 143 mph. Standing km, 28.0 sec. Fuel consumption, 22.1 mpg (at constant 75 mph).

Features: Probably the most elegant of all the Ferraris. Comprehensive instrumentation and good quality of interior furnishing. Alloy wheels. Pop-up headlamps.

FERRARI (I)

512 BBi

Identity: One of the great tiger cars, offering phenomenal handling and fire-cracker performance. Mid-engined layout, and engine is horizontally opposed 12-cylinder, hence the title Berlinetta Boxer.

Engine: Mid-mounted flat 12-cylinder with toothed belt camshaft drive and twin cams each side. Injection for engine introduced Frankfurt 1981. Bore, 82 mm, stroke 78 mm; capacity 4943 cc. Power, 335 bhp (250 kW) at 6000 rpm; torque 326 lb ft (451 Nm) at 4200 rpm.

Transmission: Rear-wheel drive; five-speed manual gearbox (no automatic version). Engine revs freely to 7000 rpm, making over 100 mph available in third. Top gear mph at 1000 rpm: 27.3.

Suspension: Front, independent, wishbones and coil springs; telescopic dampers. Anti-roll bar. Rear, independent, wishbones and coil springs; telescopic dampers. Anti-roll bar.

Steering: ZF rack and pinion.

Brakes: Discs front and rear (vented at front); servo-assisted.

Tyres: 215/70 VR 15 (front); 225/70 VR 15 (rear).

Dimensions: Length 4400 mm (173 in), width 1830 mm (72 in), height 1120 mm (44 in), wheelbase 2500 mm (98 in).

Unladen weight: 1555 kg (3425 lb).

Performance: Maximum speed, 163 mph. 0 to 60 mph, 6.2 sec. Fuel consumption, 18.7 mpg (at constant 75 mph). Note: Carburettor version tested 1978; injection version likely to be considerably faster.

Features: Outstanding combination of speed and road behaviour, but severely limited accommodation—a 'luggage in advance' car.

Identity: Derived from former 131 model, with major revisions for better safety, trim, finish and comfort. Also 1600 in some markets; UK 2-litre only.

Engine: Front-mounted four-cylinder with in-line layout and twin belt-driven overhead camshafts. Weber twin-choke carb. Bore, 84 mm, stroke 90 mm; capacity 1995 cc. Power, 113 bhp (85 kW) at 5600 rpm; torque 123 lb ft. (170 Nm) at 3700 rpm.

Transmission: Rear-wheel drive; five-speed gearbox standard; three-speed automatic optional. Final drive 3.73 (manual), 3.42 (automatic). Top gear mph at 1000 rpm: 22.1.

Suspension: Front, independent, wishbones and coil springs; telescopic gas-filled dampers; anti-roll bar. Rear, live axle on lower radius arms, upper semi-trailing links; coil springs; gas-filled dampers.

Steering: Recirculating ball, power assisted.

Brakes: Discs front, drums rear, servo-assisted.

Tyres: 185/65 R 14.

Dimensions: Length 4450 mm (175 in), width 1650 mm (65 in), height 1420 mm (56 in), wheelbase 2560 mm (101 in).

Unladen weight: 1180 kg (2601 lb).

Performance: Maximum speed, 106 mph. 0 to 60 mph, 11.6 sec. Fuel consumption, 28.0 mpg (at constant 75 mph).

Features: Roomy saloon with good equipment including central locking, electric front window lifts, stereo radio; interior light delay; concealed visors.

Identity: Chunky and distinctively styled small car with ingenious folding rear seat provisions and generous space for a compact economy car. Two side doors, and deep rear hatchback giving almost estate car load facility.

Engine: Front-mounted transverse four-cylinder with pushrod ohv, and Weber carb. Alloy head on cast iron block. Bore, 65 mm, stroke 69 mm; capacity 903 cc. Power, 45 bhp (34 kW) at 5600 rpm; torque 47 lb ft. (65 Nm) at 3000 rpm.

Transmission: Front-wheel drive; four speed gearbox and helical spur final drive; no automatic transmission available. Top gear mph at 1000 rpm: 15.8.

Suspension: Front, independent, MacPherson struts; coil springs and telescopic dampers. Anti-roll bar. Rear, dead beam axle on semi-elliptic leaf springs; telescopic dampers.

Steering: Rack and pinion.

Brakes: Discs front, drums rear, servo-assisted.

Tyres: 135 SR 12.

Dimensions: Length 3378 mm (133 in), width 1461 mm (57.5 in), height 1441 mm (57 in), wheelbase 2159 mm (85 in).

Unladen weight: 701 kg (1546 lb).

Performance: Maximum speed, 86 mph. 0 to 60 mph, 16.2 sec. Fuel consumption, 40.1 mpg (at constant 75 mph).

Features: Wrap-round moulded resin bumpers continued along sides for protection from car park knocks. Simple, functional styling and boxy shape, but quite efficient use of space.

FIAT (I)   Pininfarina Spidereuropa

Identity: Attractive two-seater convertible derived from the former 124 model, and wholly built by Pininfarina. Launched Geneva 1982, with Fiat 2-litre engine, five-speed gearbox and disc brakes all round.

Engine: Front-mounted four-cylinder with twin belt-driven ohc. Electronic fuel injection. Electronic ignition. Alloy head. Bore, 84 mm, stroke 90 mm; capacity 1995 cc. Power, 121 bhp (90 kW) at 5300 rpm; torque 124 lb ft (172 Nm) at 3500 rpm.

Transmission: Rear-wheel drive; five-speed manual gearbox. Top gear mph at 1000 rpm: 20.1.

Suspension: Front, independent, wishbones and coil springs; telescopic dampers. Anti-roll bar. Rear, live axle on longitudinal links with Panhard rod. Coil springs and telescopic dampers.

Steering: Worm and peg.

Brakes: Discs front and rear, servo-assisted.

Tyres: 185/60 SR 14.

Dimensions: Length 4140 mm (163 in), width 1615 mm (100 in), height 1250 mm (49 in), wheelbase 2280 mm (89.8 in).

Unladen weight: 1050 kg (2315 lb).

Performance (Works): Maximum speed, 112 mph. 0 to 60 mph, 10 sec. Fuel consumption, 31.4 mpg (at constant 75 mph).

Features: Elderly but sound basic design, with modern refinements to make this an appealing addition to the select convertible market. Two seats, with some luggage space in trough behind, plus separate lockable boot.

Identity: Additional, high performance version of Strada (Ritmo outside Britain), with twin ohc engine. Available in this form only with three-door body. Look for the spoilers at front and rear, and distinctive alloy wheels which distinguish this from ordinary Strada.

Engine: Front-mounted four-cylinder with twin ohc driven by toothed belt. Engine mounted transversely, and has Weber twin-choke carb, and electronic breakerless ignition. Bore, 84 mm, stroke 71.5 mm; capacity 1585 cc. Power, 105 bhp (78 kW) at 6100 rpm; torque 98.4 lb ft (136 Nm) at 4000 rpm.

Transmission: Front-wheel drive; five-speed manual gearbox standard (no automatic option). Helical spur final drive. Top gear mph at 1000 rpm: 18.4.

Suspension: Front, independent, MacPherson struts; coil springs and telescopic dampers. Anti-roll bar. Rear, independent, MacPherson struts and transverse leaf spring; telescopic dampers. Leaf spring provides anti-roll effect.

Steering: Rack and pinion.

Brakes: Discs front, drums rear, servo-assisted.

Tyres: 185/60 HR 14.

Dimensions: Length 3937 mm (155 in), width 1651 mm (65 in), height 1340 mm (55.1 in), wheelbase 2449 mm (96.4 in).

Unladen weight: 931 kg (2051 lb).

Performance: Maximum speed, 102 mph. 0 to 60 mph, 10.5 sec. Fuel consumption, 32.1 mpg (at constant 75 mph).

Features: Old facia design as on previous Strada, but up-dated and given extra instruments. Sports wheel. Snug seats with good side support; separate rear seats. Three-door hatchback body.

FIAT (I)   XI/9 1500

Identity: Delightful mid-engined two-seater with removable targa panel; car offers safe, fun motoring with exceptionally good roadholding. Poor engine access one of the few drawbacks. Larger engine version with five-speed gearbox available.

Engine: Mid-mounted four-cylinder with belt-driven ohc, and Weber twin-choke carb. Compression 9.2-to-1. Bore, 86.4 mm, stroke 63.9 mm; capacity 1498 cc. Power, 85 bhp (63 kW) at 6000 rpm; torque 87 lb ft (120 Nm) at 3200 rpm.

Transmission: Rear-wheel drive; five-speed manual gearbox (no automatic version available). All gears indirect, fifth geared-up. Top gear mph at 1000 rpm: 18.3.

Suspension: Front, independent, MacPherson struts, coil springs and telescopic dampers. Rear, independent, MacPherson struts, coil springs and telescopic dampers. No anti-roll bar front or rear—yet little roll.

Steering: Rack and pinion.

Brakes: Discs front and rear; no servo.

Tyres: 165/70 SR 13.

Dimensions: Length 1970 mm (156 in), width 1570 mm (62 in), height 1180 mm (46.5 in), wheelbase 2204 mm (86.8 in).

Unladen weight: 912 kg (2010 lb).

Performance: Maximum speed, 106 mph. 0 to 60 mph, 11.0 sec. Fuel consumption, 36.8 mpg (at constant 75 mph).

Features: Stereo radio and alloy wheels standard. Small luggage space front and rear, and detachable roof panel restows at front. Pop-up headlamps. Automatic choke.

FORD (D) Capri 2.8i

Identity: Top model in the ever-popular Capri range, made in Germany, and since end of 1981 equipped with 2.8-litre Cologne engine, with fuel injection.

Engine: Front-mounted V6-cylinder with Bosch K-Jetronic fuel injection. Cast iron heads and block; breakerless ignition. Bore, 93 mm, stroke 68.5 mm; capacity 2792 cc. Power, 160 bhp (119 kW) at 5700 rpm; torque 162 lb ft (224 Nm) at 4200 rpm.

Transmission: Rear-wheel drive; five-speed gearbox. No automatic option. Hypoid bevel final drive, ratio 3.09-to-1. Top gear mph at 1000 rpm: 25.6.

Suspension: Front, independent, MacPherson struts; transverse links and anti-roll bar. Coil springs and telescopic gas-filled dampers. Rear, live axle on semi-elliptic single leaf springs; telescopic gas-filled dampers. Anti-roll bar.

Steering: Rack and pinion, with power assistance.

Brakes: Vented discs front, drums rear, servo-assisted.

Tyres: 205/60 VR 13.

Dimensions: Length 4352 mm (171 in), width 1702 mm (67 in), height 1295 mm (51 in), wheelbase 2565 mm (101 in).

Unladen weight: 1190 kg (2620 lb).

Performance: Maximum speed, 127 mph. 0 to 60 mph, 7.9 sec. Fuel consumption, 30.1 mpg (at constant 70 mph).

Features: Large spoiler below front bumper and on rear door. Two door hatchback body with individual folding rear seats. Loud check upholstery. Distinctive alloy wheels. A straightforward and enjoyable performance car, best on long, fast journeys.

FORD (GB)   Cortina Crusader 2.0 GL

Identity: Special edition of Cortina produced in large volume to boost demand in final months before Sierra introduction. Crusader name on back and distinctive double lines at waist level.

Engine: Front-mounted four-cylinder with ohc driven by toothed belt. Cast iron head and block. Ford twin-choke carb. Bore, 90.8 mm, stroke 77 mm; capacity 1993 cc. Power, 101 bhp (75 kW) at 5200 rpm; torque 112 lb ft (155 Nm) at 4000 rpm.

Transmission: Rear-wheel drive; four-speed manual gearbox; three-speed automatic available. Top gear mph at 1000 rpm: 17.9.

Suspension: Front, independent, MacPherson struts; coil springs and telescopic dampers. Anti-roll bar. Rear, live axle on trailing and semi-trailing arms; coil springs and telescopic dampers. Anti-roll bar.

Steering: Rack and pinion.

Brakes: Discs front, drums rear, servo-assisted.

Tyres: 155 SR 13.

Dimensions: Length 4379 mm (172 in), width 1699 mm (67 in), height 1361 mm (53.6 in), wheelbase 2578 mm (101.5 in).

Unladen weight: 1009 kg (2219 lb).

Performance: Maximum speed, 102 mph. 0 to 60 mph, 10.6 sec. Fuel consumption, 28.8 mpg (at constant 75 mph).

Features: Very well finished inside for large production model, with velour upholstery and polished wood trim. Simple, sound design, very easy to drive, and capacious boot. Estate car was also available. Final build, September 1982.

FORD (GB, D)   Escort XR3i

Identity: Fastest version of the Escort line-up, with spoilers at front and rear, and since September 1982 with injection version of CVH 1600 engine. Five-speed gearbox introduced March 1982. Generally good road behaviour, and impressive performance.

Engine: Front-mounted four-cylinder with overhead camshaft driven by toothed belt. Transverse installation. Electronic ignition; K-Jetronic injection. Bore, 80 mm, stroke 79.5 mm; capacity 1593 cc. Power, 103 bhp (77 kW) at 6000 rpm; torque 100 lb ft (138 Nm) at 4800 rpm.

Transmission: Front-wheel drive; five-speed manual gearbox—no automatic option. Top gear mph at 1000 rpm: 20.1.

Suspension: Front, independent, MacPherson struts; coil springs and Bilstein gas telescopic dampers. Anti-roll bar. Rear, independent, MacPherson struts; varying rate coil springs and Bilstein gas telescopic dampers.

Steering: Rack and pinion.

Brakes: Vented discs front, drums rear, servo-assisted.

Tyres: 185/60 HR 14.

Dimensions: Length 4059 mm (160 in), width 1588 mm (62.5 in), height 1336 mm (52.6 in), wheelbase 2398 mm (94.5 in).

Unladen weight: 925 kg (2040 lb).

Performance (Works): Maximum speed, 116 mph. 0 to 60 mph, 9.7 sec. Fuel consumption, 34.9 mpg (at constant 75 mph).

Features: High-back seats. Two-door body with hatchback tail. Distinctive multi-hole alloy wheels. Electric window lifts and central locking available.

Identity: Fast and sporty version of Ford's small fwd transverse-engined two-door hatchback, launched September 1981. Special seats, steering wheel and facia, and spoilers front and rear are identifying features—plus distinctive alloy wheels.

Engine: Front-mounted transverse four-cylinder with pushrod valve gear, but Weber carb, electronic ignition and 9-to-1 compression. Bore, 81 mm, stroke 77.6 mm; capacity 1598 cc. Power, 84 bhp (63 kW) at 5500 rpm; torque 91 lb ft (126 Nm) at 5500 rpm.

Transmission: Front-wheel drive; four-speed gearbox (no automatic version). Top gear mph at 1000 rpm: 18.5.

Suspension: Front, independent, MacPherson struts; coil springs and telescopic dampers. Rear, dead beam axle on trailing links, with Panhard rod. Coil springs and telescopic dampers. Anti-roll bar.

Steering: Rack and pinion.

Brakes: Vented discs, front, drums rear, servo-assisted.

Tyres: 185/60 HR 13.

Dimensions: Length 3718 mm (146 in), width 1580 mm (62 in), height 1370 mm (54 in), wheelbase 2296 mm (90.4 in).

Unladen weight: 839 kg (1848 lb).

Performance: Maximum speed, 104 mph. 0 to 60 mph, 9.4 sec. Fuel consumption, 32.8 mpg (at constant 75 mph).

Features: Very eager and responsive car to drive, but noisy at speed; not a motorway car. Extras include tilting glass sunroof. Suspension is lower than ordinary Fiesta.

Identity: Top model in the luxury range from Ford, with most powerful of the available engines. Granada range starts with 2-litre 4-cylinder, and V6 is available as 2.3-litre or 2.8-litre with carb. or fuel injection. From Paris 1982, diesel engine (Peugeot) uprated to 2.5-litre.

Engine: Front-mounted V6-cylinder with pushrod ohv. Bosch K-Jetronic fuel injection. Compression ratio 9.2-to.1. Bore, 93 mm, stroke 68.5 mm; capacity 2792 cc. Power, 135 bhp (101 kW) at 5,200 rpm; torque, 159 lb ft (220 Nm) at 3000 rpm.

Transmission: Rear-wheel drive; four-speed manual gearbox standard for 2.8 injection, but injection Ghia has three-speed automatic as standard. Top gear mph at 1000 rpm: 20.7.

Suspension: Front, independent, wishbones and coil springs; telescopic dampers. Anti-roll bar. Rear, independent, semi-trailing arms; coil springs and telescopic dampers.

Steering: Rack and pinion, power assisted.

Brakes: Vented discs front, drums rear, servo-assisted.

Tyres: 190/65 HR 390.

Dimensions: Length 4653 mm (183.2 in), width 1793 mm (70.6 in), height 1379 mm (54.3 in), wheelbase 2769 mm (109 in).

Unladen weight: 1295 kg (2854 lb).

Performance (Works): Maximum speed, 114 mph. 0 to 60 mph, 12.1 sec. Fuel consumption, 24.4 mpg (at constant 75 mph).

Features: Comfortable car, but rather fussy at speed in automatic form. Lavish equipment including alloy wheels, tinted glass, electric window lifts, headlamp washers, radio/cassette.

Identity: Redesigned for 1983, the LTD was given a more aerodynamic body and considerably down-sized, saving 900 lb weight and with overall length cut by 18 in. Six-seater three-box saloon or estate. Choice of four engines—2.3 litre 4-cyl; 3.3-litre in-line six, and 3.8-litre V6. Fourth is propane version of 2.3. unit.

Engine: Front-mounted four-cylinder with belt-driven ohc. Hydraulic tappets. Bore, 96 mm, stroke 79.4 mm; capacity 2301 cc. Power (SAE): 86 bhp (64 kW) at 4600 rpm; torque 115 lb ft (159 Nm) at 2600 rpm.

Transmission: Rear-wheel drive; four-speed manual gearbox. Three-speed automatic optional. Final drive ratio 3.45-to-1. Top gear mph at 1000 rpm: 20.4.

Suspension: Front, independent, MacPherson struts and coil springs; telescopic dampers. Anti-roll bar. Rear, live axle on trailing and semi-trailing arms; coil springs and telescopic dampers. Anti-roll bar optional.

Steering: Recirculating ball, power assisted.

Brakes: Vented discs front, drums rear, servo-assisted.

Tyres: 185/75 R 14.

Dimensions: Length 4991 mm (196.5 in), width 1803 mm (71 in), height 1361 mm (53.6 in), wheelbase 2680 mm (105.5 in).

Unladen weight: 1352 kg (2981 lb).

Performance (est.): Maximum speed, 95 mph. Fuel consumption, 24 mpg (overall).

Features: Reclining front split-bench seat. Improved anti-corrosion, using galvanised steel and zincrometal. Optional tripminder.

Identity: Fully convertible four/five seater; hood folds down into well behind back seat, and there is no fixed roll-over bar as there was on earlier model. Headlamps recessed and horizontal slatted grille with Ford badge identifies this more attractive version.

Engine: Front-mounted V8-cylinder with four-choke carb. Central camshaft. Bore, 101.6 mm, stroke 76.2 mm; capacity 4942 cc. Power (SAE): 177 bhp (132 kW) at 4200 rpm; torque 237 lb ft (328 Nm) at 2400 rpm.

Transmission: Rear-wheel drive; four-speed manual gearbox. Top gear mph at 1000 rpm: 32.3.

Suspension: Front, independent, wishbones and coil springs; telescopic dampers. Anti-roll bar. Rear, live axle on semi-elliptic leaf springs; telescopic dampers. Anti-roll bar.

Steering: Rack and pinion, power assistance optional.

Brakes: Vented discs front, drums rear, servo-assisted.

Tyres: 220/55 R 390.

Dimensions: Length 4555 mm (179.3 in), width 1755 mm (69 in), height 1310 mm (51.5 in), wheelbase 2550 mm (100.4 in).

Unladen weight: 1290 kg (2844 lb).

Performance (est.): Maximum speed, 125 mph. 0 to 60 mph, 6.9 sec. Fuel consumption, 16 mpg (overall).

Features: Dual halogen headlamps, alloy wheels, air conditioning, cruise control, and stereo radio-cassette. Hood is power operated and has glass rear window.

FORD (GB, B)

Identity: New body, with aerodynamic shape, and independent rear suspension, to replace Cortina; launched Paris 1982. Choice of four-door hatchback or estate—no saloon version. Range of engines from 1.3 to 2.8 litres. Many options, including five-speed gearbox across most of the range (standard with 2.3 diesel and petrol versions).

Engine: Front-mounted four-cylinder with belt-driven ohc; cast iron block and head. Breakerless ignition. Ford variable venturi carb. Bore, 87.7 mm, stroke 66 mm; capacity 1594 cc. Power, 75 bhp (56 kW) at 5300 rpm; torque 88 lb ft (122 Nm) at 2900 rpm.

Transmission: Rear-wheel drive; four speed manual gearbox standard. Five-speed manual, or three-speed automatic, optional. Top gear mph at 1000 rpm: 19.4 (23.7 in optional fifth).

Suspension: Front, independent, MacPherson struts; coil springs plus polyurethane auxiliary springs and bump stops; telescopic dampers. Anti-roll bar. Rear, independent, semi-trailing arms; coil springs plus polyurethane auxiliary springs and bump stops; telescopic dampers.

Steering: Rack and pinion, power assistance optional on 2.0.

Brakes: Discs front, drums rear, servo-assisted.

Tyres: 165 SR 13.

Dimensions: Length 4394 mm (173 in), width 1720 mm (67.7 in), height 1362 mm (53.6 in), wheelbase 2608 mm (102.7 in).

Unladen weight: 1070 kg (2360 lb).

Performance: Maximum speed, 101 mph (fourth). 0 to 60 mph, 13.0 sec. Fuel consumption, 37.0 mpg (at constant 75 mph).

Features: Extremely comfortable and quiet car in its class; very easy to drive. Curved facia angles instruments and minor controls towards driver. Good range of standard equipment.

FORD (GB, B)   Sierra 2.3 Ghia

Identity: So important a new model as the Sierra needs to be included here in more than one of the available permutations of engine and trim pack, so here is the luxury version.

Engine: Front-mounted V6-cylinder with pushrod ohv. Cast iron heads and block. Solex twin-choke carb. Bore, 90 mm, stroke 60 mm; capacity 2294 cc. Power, 112 bhp (84 kW) at 5300 rpm; torque 127 lb ft (176 Nm) at 3000 rpm.

Transmission: Rear-wheel drive; five-speed manual gearbox standard. Ford three-speed automatic transmission optional. Top gear mph at 1000 rpm: 20.5 (26.1 for manual car in fifth).

Suspension: Front, independent, MacPherson struts; coil springs plus polyurethane auxiliary springs and bump stops; telescopic dampers. Anti-roll bar. Rear, independent, semi-trailing arms; coil springs and polyurethane auxiliary springs and bump stops; telescopic dampers.

Steering: Rack and pinion, power assisted.

Brakes: Vented discs front, drums rear, servo-assisted.

Tyres: 185/70 HR 13.

Dimensions: Length 4394 mm (173 in), width 1720 mm (67.7 in), height 1362 mm (53.6 in), wheelbase 2608 mm (102.7 in).

Unladen weight: 1070 kg (2360 lb).

Performance (Works): Maximum speed, 113 mph. 0 to 60 mph, 11.7 sec. Fuel consumption, 29.1 mpg (at constant 75 mph).

Features: Superbly well-equipped car with letter S for Standard appearing under most items in the option list, including sunroof, central locking, halogen headlamps, split squab rear seat, driving lamps and fog lamps.

FORD (GB)   Tickford Capri 2.8T

Identity: Exciting high performance version of Ford Capri by Aston Martin Tickford, introduced Birmingham 1982, and to go on sale 1983. Big air dam with brake cooling inlets at front, rear spoiler and side fairings. Very high performance.

Engine: Front-mounted V6-cylinder with IHI turbocharger. Compression ratio 9.2-to-1. Bosch K-Jetronic injection. Bore, 93 mm, stroke 68.5 mm; capacity 2792 cc. Power, 205 bhp (153 kW) at 5000 rpm; torque 260 lb ft (360 Nm) at 3500 rpm.

Transmission: Rear-wheel drive; five-speed manual gearbox (no automatic version). Final drive ratio 3.09-to-1. Limited slip diff. standard. Top gear mph at 1000 rpm: 25.8.

Suspension: Front, independent, MacPherson struts with transverse links; coil springs and Bilstein telescopic dampers. Anti-roll bar. Rear, live axle on semi-elliptic leaf springs, and additional lateral locating linkages. Gas-filled telescopic dampers.

Steering: Rack and pinion.

Brakes: Vented discs front, solid discs rear, servo-assisted.

Tyres: 205/60 VR 13.

Dimensions: Length 4352 mm (171.4 in), width 1702 mm (67 in), height 1295 mm (51 in), wheelbase 2565 mm (101 in).

Unladen weight: 1220 kg (2690 lb).

Performance (Works): Maximum speed, 140 mph. 0 to 60 mph, 6.0 sec. Fuel consumption, 27.4 mpg (at constant 75 mph).

Features: Recaro seats trimmed in leather. Facia panel in leather and walnut. Wilton carpet. Electrically operated windows and door mirrors. Intermittent rear wipe. Boost gauge.

Identity: After years of building Fiats under licence, sold as the Polski-Fiat, this was the Polish company's first adventure into original design. Launched 1968, largely Fiat 125 based, but with five-door hatchback body.

Engine: Front-mounted four-cylinder with pushrod ohv, and in-line installation. Alloy head. 9-to-1 compression. Weber carb. Bore, 77 mm, stroke 79.5 mm; capacity 1481 cc. Power, 76 bhp (57 kW) at 5250 rpm; torque 85 lb ft (117.5 Nm) at 3300 rpm.

Transmission: Rear-wheel drive; four-speed gearbox. Hypoid bevel final drive, ratio 4.0-to-1. Top gear mph at 1000 rpm: 16.6.

Suspension: Front, independent, wishbones and coil springs; telescopic dampers. Anti-roll bar. Rear, live axle on semi-elliptic leaf springs; telescopic dampers.

Steering: Worm and roller.

Brakes: Discs front and rear, servo-assisted.

Tyres: 175 SR 13 in.

Dimensions: Length 4272 mm (168 in), width 1650 mm (65 in), height 1379 mm (54.3 in), wheelbase 2509 mm (99 in).

Unladen weight: 1020 kg (2250 lb).

Performance: Maximum speed, 91 mph. 0 to 60 mph, 17.0 sec. Fuel consumption, 30.7 mpg (at constant 75 mph).

Features: Little merit, due to obsolete design and lack of current features for improved economy, but car has appeal due to space offered in relation to price. Simple engineering facilitates home maintenance.

Identity: Developed from the original G.4, the Series IV has a more practical shape and better weather protection. Exclusive two-seater sports car with Ford power unit; tubular steel chassis with glass fibre bodywork. Supplied in major component form for home assembly.

Engine: Front-mounted four-cylinder with pushrod ohv, cross-flow layout. Weber carb. Compression 9.2-to-1. Bore, 81 mm, stroke 77.6 mm; capacity 1599 cc. Power, 88 bhp (66 kW) at 5500 rpm; torque 92 lb ft (127 Nm) at 3500 rpm.

Transmission: Rear-wheel drive; four-speed close ratio gearbox and short travel gear lever. Top gear mph at 1000 rpm: 18.1.

Suspension: Front, independent, wishbones and coil springs; telescopic dampers. Rear, live axle on trailing arms, radius rods and Panhard rod. Coil springs and telescopic dampers.

Steering: Rack and pinion.

Brakes: Discs front, drums rear.

Tyres: 165 SR 13.

Dimensions: Length 3733 mm (147 in), width 1575 mm (62 in), height 1067 mm (42 in), wheelbase 2134 mm (84 in).

Unladen weight: 558 kg (1230 lb).

Performance (est.): Maximum speed, 105 mph. Fuel consumption, 35 mpg (overall).

Features: Fixed headlamps (previous model had pop-up headlamps). Indicators built on to front apron. Alloy wheels. Removable hood and sidescreens.

HONDA (J) Accord 3-door

Identity: Three-door hatchback version of Honda's mid-range car, completely rebodied 1981 and new on British market 1982.

Engine: Front-mounted four-cylinder with alloy head and cast iron block. Transverse mounting. Belt driven ohc. Bore, 77 mm, stroke 86 mm; capacity 1602 cc. Power, 89 bhp (66 kW) at 5300 rpm; torque 95 lb ft (132 Nm) at 3500 rpm.

Transmission: Front-wheel drive; five-speed gearbox. Hondamatic three-speed semi-automatic transmission available. Top gear mph at 1000 rpm: 23.7.

Suspension: Front, independent, MacPherson struts, coil springs and telescopic dampers. Anti-roll bar. Rear, independent, MacPherson struts, coil springs and telescopic dampers; anti-roll bar.

Steering: Rack and pinion.

Brakes: Discs front, drums rear, servo-assisted.

Tyres: 165 SR 13.

Dimensions: Length 4210 mm (166 in), width 1650 mm (65 in), height 1355 mm (53.3 in), wheelbase 2450 mm (96.5 in).

Unladen weight: 949 kg (2093 lb).

Performance: Maximum speed, 95 mph (4th). 0 to 60 mph, 12.1 sec. Fuel consumption, 35.8 mpg (at constant 75 mph).

Features: Different body style from that of Quintet, but same general approach. Available as hatchback in basic and better-equipped Executive form, or as four-door saloon. Service interval and oil change indicator lights in speedometer.

HONDA (J)

Prelude

Identity: Coupé version of Accord, with two doors, separate boot. Compact size, but rather cramped in rear; strictly 2 + 2 seating.

Engine: Front-mounted four-cylinder with single belt-driven ohc. Alloy head. Engine transversely mounted. Bore, 77 mm, stroke 86 mm; capacity 1602 cc. Power, 80 bhp (60 kW) at 5300 rpm; torque 93 lb ft (129 Nm) at 3500 rpm.

Transmission: Front-wheel drive; five-speed manual gearbox; three-speed semi-automatic optional. Top gear mph at 1000 rpm: 20.7.

Suspension: Front, independent, MacPherson struts, coil springs and telescopic dampers. Rear, independent, MacPherson struts; coil springs and telescopic dampers.

Steering: Rack and pinion; power assistance optional.

Brakes: Discs front, drums rear, servo-assisted.

Tyres: 165 SR 13.

Dimensions: Length 4089 mm (161 in), width 1635 mm (64.4 in), height 1294 mm (51 in), wheelbase 2320 mm (91.3 in).

Unladen weight: 920 kg (2028 lb).

Performance: Maximum speed, 98 mph. 0 to 60 mph, 11.3 sec. Fuel consumption, 30.4 mpg (overall).

Features: Neatly finished inside and out, and generous standard equipment includes such features as electric sliding glass sunroof, with sliding screen.

HONDA (J) **Quintet**

Identity: Five-door hatchback based on Accord model, with some affinity to Triumph's Acclaim model, which is Honda derived; practical and well-equipped family car.

Engine: Front-mounted four-cylinder with single ohc, and twin-choke carb. Transverse positioning. Alloy head, cast iron block. Bore, 77 mm, stroke 86 mm; capacity 1602 cc. Power, 79 bhp (59 kW) at 5300 rpm; torque 93 lb ft (129 Nm) at 3500 rpm.

Transmission: Front-wheel drive; five-speed gearbox, and helical 4.07-to-1 final drive. Top gear mph at 1000 rpm: 20.6.

Suspension: Front, independent, MacPherson struts; coil springs and telescopic dampers; anti-roll bar. Rear, independent MacPherson struts; coil springs and telescopic dampers; anti-roll bar.

Steering: Rack and pinion.

Brakes: Discs front, drums rear, servo-assisted.

Tyres: 155 SR 13.

Dimensions: Length 4110 mm (162 in), width 1615 mm (63 in), height 1355 mm (53 in), wheelbase 2360 mm (93 in).

Unladen weight: 933 kg (2058 lb).

Performance: Maximum speed, 93 mph. 0 to 60 mph, 12.2 sec. Fuel consumption, 34.4 mpg (at constant 75 mph).

Features: Equipment includes electrically operated sunroof and radio. Split rear seat, either half folds forward for extra luggage space. Folding rear shelf goes up with back door.

HYUNDAI (KOREA)   Pony 1400TLS

Identity: Very conventional design with chunky front, four headlamps in square surrounds; the main merit of this Korean import is its competitive value. Cheaper models available, with 1238 cc engine. Hatchback or four-door saloon body.

Engine: Front-mounted four-cylinder built under licence from Mitsubishi. Alloy head, cast iron block. Chain driven ohc. Bore, 73 mm, stroke 86 mm; capacity 1439 cc. Power, 67 bhp (50 kW) at 6300 rpm; torque 40.4 lb ft (56 Nm) at 4000 rpm.

Transmission: Rear-wheel drive; four-speed gearbox, and hypoid live axle with 3.89-to-1 ratio. Automatic transmission available. Top gear mph at 1000 rpm: 17.05.

Suspension: Front, independent, MacPherson struts; coil springs and telescopic dampers; anti-roll bar. Rear, live axle on semi-elliptic leaf springs. Telescopic dampers.

Steering: Recirculating ball.

Brakes: Discs front, drums rear, servo-assisted.

Tyres: 155 SR 13.

Dimensions: Length 3970 mm (156 in), width 1558 mm (61.3 in), height 1360 mm (53.6 in), wheelbase 2340 mm (92 in).

Unladen weight: 968 kg (2133 lb).

Performance: Maximum speed, 89 mph. 0 to 60 mph, 14.8 sec. Fuel consumption, 31.3 mpg (at constant 75 mph).

Features: Not a very inspiring car to drive—it feels, as it is, a very dated design, but competitive pricing makes it all worthwhile.

INNOCENTI (I)   3 Cylindres SE

Identity: Italian version of the Mini, originally equipped with BL engine and transmission, but now with Daihatsu three-cylinder—hence unusual model name. Body designed by Bertone with chunky shape and roof line curved upwards at rear.

Engine: Front-mounted three-cylinder with belt-driven ohc. Aisan carb. Bore, 76 mm, stroke 73 mm; capacity 993 cc. Power, 52 bhp (39 kW) at 5000 rpm; torque 55 lb ft (76 Nm) at 3200 rpm.

Transmission: Front-wheel drive; five-speed manual gearbox. Final drive 4.28-to-1. Top gear mph at 1000 rpm: 17.3.

Suspension: Front, independent, MacPherson struts, coil springs and telescopic dampers. Rear, independent, trailing arms and torsion bars; transverse links. Telescopic dampers.

Steering: Rack and pinion.

Brakes: Discs front, drums rear, servo-assisted.

Tyres: 155/70 SR 12.

Dimensions: Length 3160 mm (124.4 in), width 1520 mm (59.8 in), height 1370 mm (53.9), wheelbase 2045 mm (80.5 in).

Unladen weight: 670 kg (1477 lb).

Performance (Works): Maximum speed, 90 mph. 0 to 60 mph, 17.4 sec. Fuel consumption, 53.9 mpg (at constant 56 mph).

Features: Folding back seat with shelf which lifts on cords when rear hatch is opened. Split rear bench seat on top model. Full width 'Innocenti' lettering on back. Basic economy car.

JAGUAR (GB) XJ 3.4

Identity: Familiar XJ long wheelbase saloon, but with the smaller six-cylinder engine, and thus cheapest Jaguar available. Numerous detail improvements made October 1982, mainly incorporating features previously exclusive to the Daimler.

Engine: Front-mounted six-cylinder with twin chain-driven ohc. Twin SU carbs. Bore, 83 mm, stroke 106 mm; capacity 3442 cc. Power, 161 bhp (120 kW) at 5000 rpm; torque 189 lb ft. (261 Nm) at 3500 rpm.

Transmission: Rear-wheel drive; five-speed manual gearbox; three-speed automatic optional. Hypoid bevel final drive, 3.54-to-1. Top gear mph at 1000 rpm: 27.2.

Suspension: Front, independent, wishbones and coil springs; telescopic dampers. Anti-roll bar. Rear, trailing arms, wishbones and fixed length drive shafts; dual coil springs and telescopic dampers.

Steering: Rack and pinion, power assisted.

Brakes: Discs front and rear, servo-assisted.

Tyres: 70 VR 15.

Dimensions: Length 4959 mm (195.2 in), width 1770 mm (69.7 in), height 1377 mm (54 in), wheelbase 2866 mm (112.8 in).

Unladen weight: 1805 kg (3978 lb).

Performance: Maximum speed, 117 mph. 0 to 60 mph, 10.9 sec. Fuel consumption, 23.7 mpg (at constant 75 mph).

Features: Superb comfort, and very good compromise between needs for Jaguar standards of performance but also adequate economy. Very well equipped, though not quite up to the standards of dearer Jaguars.

JAGUAR (GB) XJS HE

Identity: World standard-setter for combination of performance with refinement; superb handling and ride. Close-coupled four-seater two door coupé. Convertible addition, 1983.

Engine: Front-mounted V12-cylinder with block and heads in alloy; single ohc each bank; Lucas digital fuel injection. Bore, 90 mm, stroke 70 mm; capacity 5345 cc. Power, 299 bhp (223 kW) at 5500 rpm; torque 318 lb ft (440 Nm) at 3000 rpm.

Transmission: Rear-wheel drive; GM 400 automatic three-speed transmission (no manual availability). Limited slip diff. Top gear mph at 1000 rpm: 26.9.

Suspension: Front, independent, wishbones with anti-dive geometry: Coil springs and telescopic dampers; anti-roll bar. Rear, independent, drive shafts, radius arms and bottom links; twin coil springs each side, and twin telescopic dampers; anti-roll bar.

Steering: Rack and pinion with power assistance.

Brakes: Discs front and rear, servo-assisted.

Tyres: 215/70 VR 15.

Dimensions: Length 4743 mm (187 in), width 1793 mm (70.5 in), height 1270 mm (50 in), wheelbase 2591 mm (102 in).

Unladen weight: 1735 kg (3824 lb).

Performance: Maximum speed, 153 mph. 0 to 60 mph, 6.5 sec. Fuel consumption, 22.5 mpg (at constant 75 mph).

Features: Fabulous performance, reaching 130 mph in 33 sec. High efficiency engine with 12.5-to-1 compression. Superbly equipped with air conditioning, leather upholstery, electric window lifts and central locking.

LADA (SU)   Niva

Identity: Rugged cross-country vehicle, identifiable by the unusual positioning of side and indicator lamps above the headlamps. Not a very pleasant vehicle to drive, but inexpensive for a four-wheel-drive vehicle.

Engine: Front-mounted four-cylinder with chain-driven overhead camshaft. Alloy cylinder-head. Bore, 79 mm, stroke 80 mm; capacity 1569 cc. Power, 77 bhp (57.5 kW) at 5400 rpm; torque 89 lb ft (123 Nm) at 3200 rpm.

Transmission: Four-wheel drive; four-speed gearbox with low ratio transfer box. Final drive 4.3-to-1. Top gear mph at 1000 rpm: 15.3.

Suspension: Front, live axle, wishbones and coil springs; telescopic dampers. Anti-roll bar. Rear, live axle, longitudinal links and Panhard rod; coil springs and telescopic dampers.

Steering: Worm and roller.

Brakes: Discs front, drums rear, servo-assisted.

Tyres: 6.95/16.

Dimensions: Length 3708 mm (146 in), width 1676 mm (66 in), height 1638 mm (64.5 in), wheelbase 2197 mm (86.5 in).

Unladen weight: 1150 kg (2535 lb).

Performance: Maximum speed, 77 mph. 0 to 60 mph, 22.4 sec. Fuel consumption, 23.3 mpg (at constant 75 mph).

Features: Crude but durable and practical interior. Two-door body with opening back. Good cross-country performance.

LAMBORGHINI (I)   Countach LP 500S

Identity: Exciting Italian mid-engined two-seater with vertically rising forward pivoted doors. New version with 4.75-litre engine launched Geneva 1982. Space-frame chassis, and Bertone-designed aluminium body.

Engine: Mid-mounted V12-cylinder with four chain-driven overhead camshafts. Six Weber twin-choke carbs! Alloy heads and block. Bore, 85.5 mm, stroke 69 mm; capacity 4754 cc. Power, 375 bhp (281 kW) at 7000 rpm; torque 302 lb ft (418 Nm) at 4500 rpm.

Transmission: Rear-wheel drive; five-speed manual gearbox. Hypoid bevel final drive, ratio 4.09-to-1. Top gear mph at 1000 rpm: 24.5.

Suspension: Front, independent, wishbones and coil springs; telescopic dampers. Anti-roll bar. Rear, independent, wide-base wishbones and coil springs; twin telescopic dampers each side. Anti-roll bar.

Steering: Rack and pinion.

Brakes: Vented discs front and rear, servo-assisted.

Tyres: 205/50 VR 15 (front); 345/35 VR 15 (rear).

Dimensions: Length 4140 mm (162.9 in), width 2000 mm (78.7 in), height 1070 mm (42.1 in), wheelbase 2450 mm (96.5 in).

Unladen weight: 1321 kg (2913 lb).

Performance: Maximum speed, 164 mph. 0 to 60 mph, 5.6 sec. Fuel consumption, 17.2 mpg (at constant 75 mph).

Features: Small boot at rear, and additional space with spare wheel and battery in diminutive forward compartment. Pop-up headlamps. Extravagant finish and equipment, inc. air conditioning.

Identity: New version of the Lancia small car, introduced September 1982, but differences are mainly just the fitting of electric front window lifts and sliding panel sunroof. Chunky, nippy four-door hatchback with mainly Fiat running gear, but exclusively Lancia body.

Engine: Front-mounted four-cylinder with single ohc, belt-driven; transverse mounting. Aluminium alloy head, and engine inclined forwards at 20 deg. angle for better access. Bore, 86 mm, stroke 64 mm; capacity 1498 cc. Power, 85 bhp (63 kW) at 6200 rpm; torque 90 lb ft (117.5 Nm) at 3500 rpm.

Transmission: Front-wheel drive; five-speed gearbox. No automatic version. Helical spur final drive, ratio 3.765-to-1. Top gear mph at 1000 rpm: 17.9.

Suspension: Front, independent, MacPherson struts; coil springs and telescopic dampers. Anti-roll bar. Rear, independent, MacPherson struts; coil springs and telescopic dampers. Anti-roll bar.

Steering: Rack and pinion.

Brakes: Discs front, drums rear, servo-assisted.

Tyres: 165/70 SR 13 in.

Dimensions: Length 3885 mm (153 in), width 1620 mm (64 in), height 1390 mm (54.3 in), wheelbase 2475 mm (97.4 in).

Unladen weight: 987 kg (2176 lb).

Performance: Maximum speed, 97 mph. 0 to 60 mph, 11.5 sec. Fuel consumption, 30.2 mpg (at constant 75 mph).

Features: Delightful road behaviour, with excellent cornering and precise steering. Rather crude facia design; plain inside, but well-equipped. Full instrumentation including rev counter; digital clock.

LANCIA (I)   Gamma Olgiata

Identity: Elegantly styled two-door estate by Pininfarina; world debut Paris 1982. Included here for interest although it is not a production car, but details apply also for the Lancia Gamma Coupé on which the Olgiata is based.

Engine: Front-mounted four-cylinder with horizontally opposed cylinders. Belt-driven twin ohc. Twin choke carb. Bore, 91.5 mm, stroke 76 mm; capacity 1999 cc. Power, 115 bhp (85 kW) at 5500 rpm; torque 124 lb ft (172 Nm) at 3500 rpm.

Transmission: Front-wheel drive; five-speed manual gearbox. Final drive ratio 3.7-to-1 (saloon: 4.1). Top gear mph at 1000 rpm: 20.6.

Suspension: Front, independent, MacPherson struts; coil springs and telescopic dampers. Anti-roll bar. Rear, independent, MacPherson struts and longitudinal links; coil springs and telescopic dampers.

Steering: Rack and pinion, power assisted.

Brakes: Vented discs front, solid discs rear, servo-assisted.

Tyres: 185/70 HR 14.

Dimensions: Length 4485 mm (176.5 in), width 1730 mm (68.1 in), height 1330 mm (52.4 in), wheelbase 2555 mm (100·6 in).

Unladen weight: 1270 kg (2800 lb).

Performance (Works): Maximum speed, 112 mph. 0 to 60 mph, 12.0 sec. Fuel consumption, 25.9 mpg (at constant 75 mph).

Features: Four-seater two-door with opening rear door. Darkened glass to conceal roof support posts. Wind deflector at rear to eliminate swirl and keep back window clean. Alloy wheels.

LANCIA (I)   **Prisma**

Identity: Entirely new model, launched December 1982, on UK market mid-1983. Three-box four-door saloon body, and front drive. Choice of 1300, 1500 or 1600 c.c. engines; front drive, and five-speed manual gearbox, with three-speed automatic option for 1500 only.

Engine: Front-mounted four-cylinder with twin ohc, belt-driven. Transverse mounting; alloy head. Marelli Digiplex electronic ignition. Weber carb. Compression 9.3-to-1. Bore, 84 mm, stroke 71.5 mm; capacity 1,585 c.c. Output 105 bhp (77 kW) at 5,800 rpm; torque 98 lb. ft. (135 Nm) at 3,300 rpm.

Transmission: Front-wheel drive; five-speed manual gearbox (no automatic option for 1600). Final drive ratio 3.59-to-1. Top gear mph at 1,000 rpm: 18.6.

Suspension: Front, independent, MacPherson struts; coil springs and telescopic dampers. Anti-roll bar. Rear, independent, MacPherson struts; transverse links and longitudinal reaction rod; coil springs and telescopic dampers. Anti-roll bar.

Steering: Rack and pinion.

Brakes: Discs front, and rear, servo-assisted.

Tyres: 165/65 SR 14.

Dimensions: Length 4180 mm (164.6 in.), width 1620 mm (63.8 in.), height 1385 mm (54.5 in.), wheelbase 2475 mm (97.4 in.).

Unladen weight: 975 kg (2150 lb).

Performance: Maximum speed, 111 mph. 0 to 60 mph, 10.2 sec. Fuel consumption, 33.6 mpg (at constant 75 mph).

Features: Typical Lancia attention to ride, steering and handling. Good instrumentation with check control panel for main services. Electric window lifts and central locking on 1600. Options include trip computer, sunroof, air conditioning, and individually folding rear seats (unusual on a saloon).

Identity: Three-box replacement for the Beta—hence the name, from the Italian for 'three volumes'—*tre volumi*. Sporting saloon, with remarkable facia treatment, with switches like eyes aimed towards the driver. Choice of 1600 or 2000 cc engine.

Engine: Front-mounted transverse four-cylinder with twin overhead camshafts driven by toothed belt. Breakerless ignition; Weber carburettor. Bore, 84 mm, stroke 90 mm; capacity 1995 cc. Power, 115 bhp (86 kW) at 5500 rpm; torque 129 lb ft (178 Nm) at 2800 rpm.

Transmission: Front-wheel drive; five-speed gearbox, but rather low overall gearing. Three-speed automatic available. Hypoid bevel final drive, ratio 3.79-to-1. Top gear mph at 1000 rpm: 19.3.

Suspension: Front, independent, MacPherson struts; coil springs and telescopic dampers. Anti-roll bar. Rear, independent, MacPherson struts; coil springs and telescopic dampers. Anti-roll bar.

Steering: Rack and pinion: power assisted.

Brakes: Discs front and rear, servo-assisted.

Tyres: 185/65 HR 14 in.

Dimensions: Length 4355 mm (171.5 in), width 1706 mm (67 in), height 1400 mm (55 in), wheelbase 2540 mm (100 in).

Unladen weight: 1181 kg (2605 lb).

Performance: Maximum speed, 113 mph. 0 to 60 mph, 11.1 sec. Fuel consumption, 28.1 mpg (at constant 75 mph).

Features: Systems check light in front of driver; electric window lifts; manual action but very easy to operate sliding panel sunroof. Multifunction digital clock.

LANCIA (I)   Trevi Volumex VX

Identity: World's sole volume-production supercharged car. Different identity is revealed by VX logo on grille, and Tevi Volumex VX lettering on aluminium stripe on rear quarter, right side only. Launched Paris 1982; into export markets 1983.

Engine: Front-mounted four-cylinder with belt-driven twin ohc and (also belt-driven) induction compressor (supercharger). Compression ratio 7.5-to-1. Transverse installation. Bore, 84 mm, stroke 90 mm; capacity 1995 cc. Power, 135 bhp (99 kW) at 5500 rpm; torque 149 lb ft (206 Nm) at 3000 rpm.

Transmission: Front-wheel drive; five-speed manual gearbox (no automatic option). Final drive ratio 3.42-to-1. Top gear mph at 1000 rpm: 22.9.

Suspension: Front, independent, MacPherson struts; coil springs and telescopic dampers. Anti-roll bar. Rear, independent, MacPherson struts with transverse arms. Anti-roll bar.

Steering: Rack and pinion, power assisted.

Brakes: Discs front and rear, servo-assisted.

Tyres: 185/65 HR 14. Pirelli P6.

Dimensions: Length 4355mm (171.5 in), width 1706 mm (67.2 in), height 1400 mm (55.1 in), wheelbase 2540 mm (100 in).

Unladen weight: 1195 kg (2635 lb).

Performance (Works): Maximum speed, 118 mph. 0 to 60 mph, 9.6 sec. Fuel consumption, 29.4 mpg (at constant 75 mph).

Features: Improved seats with upholstery in Zegna wool cloth, and recesses on rear to give extra rear legroom. Front door pockets. Supercharger zone marked on rev counter. Otherwise largely as Trevi.

LAND-ROVER (GB)　　V8 County Estate Car

Identity: Top version of the Land-Rover, with same engine as in Range Rover, and permanent four-wheel drive. Better equipment and trim inside all included as part of the County package. Impressive cross-country ability, but no match for Range Rover on the road.

Engine: Front-mounted V8-cylinder with alloy heads and block. Hydraulic tappets. Twin Zenith-Stromberg carbs. Bore, 88.9 mm, stroke 71.1 mm; capacity 3528 cc. Power, 91 bhp (68 kW) at 3500 rpm; torque 166 lb ft (226 Nm) at 2000 rpm.

Transmission: Four-wheel drive; lockable centre diff, as on Range Rover, in addition to front and rear diffs. Top gear mph at 1000 rpm: 15.0.

Suspension: Front, live axle on semi-elliptic leaf springs; telescopic dampers. Rear, live axle on semi-elliptic leaf springs; telescopic dampers.

Steering: Recirculating ball.

Brakes: Drums front and rear, servo-assisted.

Tyres: 7.50-16.

Dimensions: Length 4445 mm (175 in), width 1690 mm (66.5 in), height 1920 mm (75.6 in), wheelbase 2768 mm (109 in).

Unladen weight: 1805 kg (3980 lb).

Performance (est.): Maximum speed, 75 mph. Fuel consumption, 14 mpg (overall).

Features: Plain but functional interior, all of tough, durable materials. Four-door estate car body, with folding step for each door. Almost unbeatable cross-country performance.

LINCOLN (USA)   Continental Mark VI

Identity: Big American luxury car, available as four-door saloon or two-door coupé. Distinctive radiator grille with square surround and vertical ribbing. Headlamps concealed beneath roll-up flaps. First launched 1979.

Engine: Front-mounted V8-cylinder with hydraulic tappets, electronic fuel injection and electronic ignition. Compression 8.4-to-1. Bore, 101.6 mm, stroke 76.2 mm; capacity 4942 cc. Power (SAE): 134 bhp (100 kW) at 3400 rpm; torque 228 lb ft (315 Nm) at 2200 rpm.

Transmission: Rear-wheel drive; four-speed automatic transmission standard, with steering column-mounted selector. Top gear mph at 1000 rpm: 25.5.

Suspension: Front, independent, wishbones and coil springs; nitrogen filled telescopic dampers. Anti-roll bar. Rear, live axle on trailing and semi-trailing links; coil springs and telescopic dampers. Anti-roll bar optional.

Steering: Recirculating ball, power assisted.

Brakes: Vented discs front, drums rear, servo-assisted.

Tyres: 205/75 R 15.

Dimensions: Length 5565 mm (219 in), width 1985 mm (78 in), height 1420 mm (56 in), wheelbase 2980 mm (117.3 in).

Unladen weight: 1815 kg (4000 lb).

Performance (est.): Maximum speed, 105 mph. Fuel consumption, 14 mpg (overall).

Features: Lavishly equipped with most luxury fittings included as standard; limited slip diff. optional.

LOTUS (GB)   Eclat Excel

Identity: New version of Eclat, introduced end of September 1982. Body shape revised, especially at front, and new rear suspension to give still better roadholding. Reshaped roof line gives more rear seat headroom. Efficient, sporting 2 + 2.

Engine: Front-mounted four-cylinder with 4 valves per cylinder. Alloy head and block; wet liners. Belt-driven twin ohc. Bore, 95.3 mm, stroke 76.2 mm; capacity 2174 cc. Power, 160 bhp (119 kW) at 6500 rpm; torque 160 lb ft (221 Nm) at 5000 rpm.

Transmission: Rear-wheel drive; five-speed gearbox standard, automatic transmission optional. Hypoid bevel final drive, 4.1-to-1. Top gear mph at 1000 rpm: 20.8.

Suspension: Front, independent, wishbones and coil springs; telescopic dampers. Anti-roll bar. Rear, independent, wishbones and coil springs; telescopic dampers.

Steering: Rack and pinion, power assistance optional.

Brakes: Vented discs front and rear, servo-assisted.

Tyres: 205/60 VR 14.

Dimensions: Length 4376 mm (172.3 in), width 1816 mm (71.5 in), height 1207 mm (40.4 in), wheelbase 2483 mm (97.8 in).

Unladen weight: 1135 kg (2500 lb).

Performance (Works): Maximum speed, 134 mph. 0 to 60 mph, 7.0 sec. Fuel consumption, 29.4 mpg (at constant 75 mph).

Features: Glass fibre 2 + 2 body, with high standard of colour finish. Pop-up headlamps. Alloy wheels. Spoiler with four openings below bumper distinguishes the Excel from previous model.

LOTUS (GB)   Elite 2.2

Identity: Glass fibre bodied 2+2, similar to Eclat but with squarer tail. Pop-up headlamps. Engine enlarged to 2.2-litre May 1980.

Engine: Front-mounted four-cylinder with four valves per cylinder. Alloy head and block; wet liners. Belt-driven twin ohc. Bore, 95.3 mm, stroke 76.2 mm; capacity 2174 cc. Power, 160 bhp (119 kW) at 6500 rpm; torque 160 lb ft (221 Nm) at 5000 rpm.

Transmission: Rear-wheel drive; five-speed gearbox standard. Automatic transmission option. Hypoid final drive, 4.1-to-1 or 3.73. Top gear mph at 1000 rpm: 22.5 with 3.73 final drive.

Suspension: Front, independent, wishbones and coil springs; telescopic dampers. Anti-roll bar. Rear, independent, wishbones and coil springs; telescopic dampers.

Steering: Rack and pinion, power assistance optional.

Brakes: Vented discs front and rear, servo-assisted.

Tyres: 205/60 VR 14.

Dimensions: Length 4376 mm (172.3 in), width 1816 mm (71.5 in), height 1207 mm (40.4 in), wheelbase 2483 mm (97.8 in).

Unladen weight: 1120 kg (2469 lb).

Performance: Maximum speed, 127 mph. 0 to 60 mph, 7.5 sec. Fuel consumption, 20.6 mpg (overall).

Features: Electric window lifts. Rear window hinged to lift upwards for luggage loading, and equipped with wash/wipe. Single central front wiper. Slightly more practical rear accommodation.

LOTUS (GB) Esprit Turbo

Identity: Launched first as a limited edition model, but now in standard Lotus programme. Mid-engined two-seater, turbocharged, and with aerodynamic glass fibre body. Pop-up headlamps.

Engine: Mid-mounted four-cylinder with twin ohc, belt-driven. Twin Dellorto carbs. Garrett T3 turbocharger. Alloy head and block. 4 valves per cylinder. Bore, 95.3 mm, stroke 76.2 mm; capacity 2174 cc. Power, 210 bhp (154 kW) at 6000 rpm; torque 200 lb ft (280 Nm) at 4500 rpm.

Transmission: Rear-wheel drive; five-speed manual gearbox. No automatic option. Final drive 4.38-to-1. Top gear mph at 1000 rpm: 22.4.

Suspension: Front, independent, wishbones and coil springs; telescopic dampers. Anti-roll bar. Rear, independent, trailing arms and lateral links. Coil springs and telescopic dampers, coaxial with springs.

Steering: Rack and pinion.

Brakes: Vented discs front, solid discs (inboard) rear, servo-assisted.

Tyres: 195/60 VR 15 (front); 235/60 VR 15 (rear).

Dimensions: Length 4191 mm (165 in), width 1854 mm (73 in), height 1118 mm (44 in), wheelbase 2438 mm (96 in).

Unladen weight: 1220 kg (2690 lb).

Performance: Maximum speed, 148 mph. 0 to 60 mph, 6.1 sec. Fuel consumption, 33.3 mpg (at constant 75 mph).

Features: Very well finished, and fully equipped with air conditioning standard. Impressive handling. Leather seats and trim; alloy wheels. Spoilers front and rear.

MASERATI (I)   **Biturbo**

Identity: Addition to Maserati range, launched end 1981. Two-door five-seater body with chunky front, oblong lamps. Turbocharged V6 engine.

Engine: Front-mounted V6-cylinder with three valves per cylinder, two ohc each bank. Toothed belt camshaft drive. Compression 7.8-to-1. Twin-choke Weber carb, with twin turbochargers. Bore, 82 mm, stroke 63 mm; capacity 1996 cc. Power, 178 bhp (132.5 kW) at 6000 rpm; torque 184 lb ft (255 Nm) at 3500 rpm.

Transmission: Rear-wheel drive; five-speed gearbox. ZF three-speed automatic optional. Limited slip diff. Top gear mph at 1000 rpm: 20.8.

Suspension: Front, independent, wishbones and coil springs; telescopic dampers. Anti-roll bar. Rear, independent, semi-trailing arms; coil springs and telescopic dampers.

Steering: Rack and pinion, power assisted.

Brakes: Discs front and rear, servo-assisted.

Tyres: 195/60 HR.

Dimensions: Length 4155 mm (163.5 in), width 1715 mm (67.5 in), height 1305 mm (51.4 in), wheelbase 2515 mm (99.0 in).

Unladen weight: 1085 kg (2392 lb).

Performance (Works): Maximum speed, 134 mph. 0 to 60 mph, 6.5 sec. Fuel consumption, 16.6 mpg (touring).

Features: High performance, with good power-weight ratio. Typical Maserati mixture of quality spoilt by slight lack of neatness and uninspired design. Alloy wheels.

MASERATI (I)   Khamsin

Identity: Elegantly-styled 2 + 2-seater coupé, first seen as prototype at Turin, 1972. Conventional front engine, rear drive layout.

Engine: Front-mounted V8-cylinder with twin ohc, chain driven. Dry sump lubrication. Four-choke Weber carb. Bore, 93.9 mm, stroke 89 mm; capacity 4930 cc. Power, 320 bhp (239 kW) at 5500 rpm; torque 354 lb ft (489 Nm) at 4000 rpm.

Transmission: Rear-wheel drive; ZF five-speed gearbox. Limited slip diff. Final drive ratio 3.31-to-1. Top gear mph at 1000 rpm: 26.7.

Suspension: Front, independent, wishbones and coil springs; telescopic dampers. Anti-roll bar. Rear, independent, wishbones and coil springs; telescopic dampers. Anti-roll bar.

Steering: Rack and pinion, Citroen high response Varipower system.

Brakes: Vented discs front and rear, servo-assisted.

Tyres: 215/70 VR 15.

Dimensions: Length 4400 mm (173 in), width 1805 mm (71 in), height 1140 mm (45 in), wheelbase 2550 mm (100.4 in).

Unladen weight: 1680 kg (3704 lb).

Performance: Maximum speed, 160 mph. 0 to 60 mph, 6.5 sec.. Fuel consumption, 14.3 mpg (overall).

Features: Very sensitive and progressive steering takes a little while to familiarise, but when the driver is 'at home' with the car the handling is excellent, and coupled with terrific performance it is spectacularly fast transport. Noisy. Well-equipped.

MASERATI (I)   Kyalami

Identity: Two very similar Maseratis are produced—the Kyalami two-door 2+2, and the Quattroporte four-door limousine five-seater, which has 4.1-litre V8 engine. More exciting version (details here) is the Kyalami, with 4.9-litre V8.

Engine: Front-mounted V8-cylinder with twin chain-driven ohc. 4-choke Weber carb. Alloy block and heads. Bore, 93.9 mm, stroke 89 mm; capacity 4930 cc. Power, 276 bhp (206 kW) at 5600 rpm; torque 284 lb ft (392 Nm) at 3000 rpm.

Transmission: Rear-wheel drive; five-speed manual gearbox. Three-speed automatic optional. Limited slip diff. Top gear mph at 1000 rpm: 26.1.

Suspension: Front, independent, wishbones and coil springs; telescopic dampers. Anti-roll bar. Rear, independent, trailing arms, transverse links and half shafts; coil springs and telescopic dampers. Anti-roll bar.

Steering: Rack and pinion, power assisted.

Brakes: Vented discs front and rear, servo-assisted.

Tyres: 205/70 VR 15.

Dimensions: Length 4572 mm (180 in), width 1849 mm (72.8 in), height 1270 mm (50 in), wheelbase 2598 mm (102.3 in).

Unladen weight: 1750 kg (3857 lb).

Performance: Maximum speed, 147 mph. 0 to 60 mph, 7.6 sec. Fuel consumption, 15.3 mpg (overall).

Features: Air conditioning, electric window lifts and tinted glass all standard. Luxurious interior trim. Performance and sporting handling combined with luxury car appeal.

MASERATI (I)   Merak

Identity: High performance 2+2-seater coupé with mid-engined layout, and choice of 2-litre or 3-litre engine (both V6). Details here are for the Merak SS, which has the 3-litre unit. Sloping rear quarter struts are identifying feature.

Engine: Mid-mounted V6-cylinder with twin ohc each bank. Alloy heads and block. Weber 44 twin-choke carb. Bore, 91.6 mm, stroke 75 mm; capacity 2965 cc. Power, 205 bhp (153 kW) at 6000 rpm; torque 184 lb ft (255 Nm) at 4500 rpm.

Transmission: Rear-wheel drive; five-speed gearbox. No automatic option. Ratio 4.37-to-1. Top gear mph at 1000 rpm: 24.5.

Suspension: Front, independent, wishbones and coil springs; telescopic dampers. Anti-roll bar. Rear, independent, wishbones and coil springs; telescopic dampers. Anti-roll bar.

Steering: Rack and pinion.

Brakes: Vented discs front and rear, servo-assisted.

Tyres: Front, 195/70 VR 15; rear, 215/70 VR 15.

Dimensions: Length 4335 mm (170.7 in), width 1770 mm (69.7 in), height 1135 mm (44.7 in) wheelbase 2600 mm (102 in).

Unladen weight: 1350 kg (2976 lb).

Performance: Maximum speed, 143 mph. 0 to 60 mph, 7.7 sec. Fuel consumption, 17.9 mpg (overall).

Features: Rather cramped, and restricted visibility, but a very exciting car to drive. Well-equipped. Alloy wheels.

MAZDA (J)

323 1500 GT

Identity: Fastest version of the 323 hatchback range, available only with three doors. Tuned version of 1500 engine. The GT is supplemented by a GTS with slightly better equipment in some markets.

Engine: Front-mounted four-cylinder with chain driven ohc. Alloy head. Transverse installation. Two Hitachi twin-choke carbs. Bore, 77 mm, stroke 80 mm; capacity 1490 cc. Power, 85 bhp (63 kW) at 6000 rpm; torque 88 lb ft (121 Nm) at 3200 rpm.

Transmission: Front-wheel drive; five-speed manual gearbox. No automatic option for GT, but automatic is available with 1490 engine. Top gear mph at 1000 rpm: 22.1.

Suspension: Front, independent, MacPherson struts; coil springs and telescopic dampers. Anti-roll bar. Rear, independent, MacPherson struts with trailing and transverse arms; coil springs and telescopic dampers. Anti-roll bar.

Steering: Rack and pinion.

Brakes: Discs front, drums rear, servo-assisted.

Tyres: 175/70 SR 13.

Dimensions: Length 3955 mm (155.7 in), width 1630 mm (64.2 in), height 1375 mm (54.1 in), wheelbase 2365 mm (93.1 in).

Unladen weight: 850 kg (1873 lb).

Performance: Maximum speed, 101 mph. 0 to 60 mph, 10.7 sec. Fuel consumption, 38.7 mpg (at constant 75 mph).

Features: Rear and front seats have head restraints. Rear seats fold for extra luggage space. Sports steering wheel with adjustable rake. Sunroof, digital clock and rev counter standard.

MAZDA (J)

Identity: Still not available on British market, but included here as a car of intriguing design. Dates back to the Mazda Cosmo of Frankfurt 1975, but new version launched October 1981. Choice of diesel or Wankel engine, or four-cyl. (detailed below).

Engine: Front-mounted four-cylinder with chain driven single ohc. Alloy head. Bore, 80mm, stroke 98 mm; capacity 1970 cc. Power, 88 bhp (66 kW) at 5000 rpm; torque 114 lb ft (157 Nm) at 2600 rpm.

Transmission: Rear-wheel drive; five-speed manual gearbox. Three-speed automatic optional. Top gear mph at 1000 rpm: 22.7.

Suspension: Front, independent, MacPherson struts; coil springs and telescopic dampers. Anti-roll bar. Rear, independent, semi-trailing arms; coil springs and telescopic dampers. Anti-roll bar.

Steering: Rack and pinion, varying ratio; power assisted.

Brakes: Vented discs front, solid discs rear, servo-assisted.

Tyres: 195/70 HR 14.

Dimensions: Length 4640 mm (182.6 in), width 1690 mm (66.5 in), height 1355 mm (53.3 in), wheelbase 2615mm (103 in).

Unladen weight: 1160 kg (2557 lb).

Performance (Works): Maximum speed, 106 mph. Fuel consumption (estimated): 23 mpg (overall).

Features: Multiple push button switches either side of instrument nascelle. Centre console. Halogen headlamps. Electric windows. Air conditioning on S spec.

Identity: Despite all the problems of the past, Mazda persisted with the Wankel rotary engine, and use it to power their sleekly styled two-door coupé with opening rear hatch. Close-coupled 2 + 2 seat capacity, and considerable sporting appeal.

Engine: Front-mounted twin-rotor Wankel of die-cast alloy construction, with steel liners. Breakerless ignition; Nippon carburettor. Chamber capacity, 573 cc. Equivalent engine capacity 2292 cc. Power, 115 bhp (86 kW) at 6000 rpm; torque 112 lb ft (155 Nm) at 4000 rpm.

Transmission: Rear-wheel drive; five-speed manual gearbox (no automatic version). Hypoid bevel final drive, 3.909-to-1. Top gear mph at 1000 rpm: 21.0.

Suspension: Front, independent, MacPherson struts, coil springs and telescopic dampers. Anti-roll bar. Rear, live axle on trailing arms, with Watt linkage. Coil springs and telescopic dampers. Anti-roll bar.

Steering: Recirculating ball.

Brakes: Discs front and rear, servo-assisted.

Tyres: 185/70 HR 13.

Dimensions: Length 4323 mm (170 in), width 1675 mm (66 in), height 1260 mm (49.6 in), wheelbase 2420 mm (95.3 in).

Unladen weight: 1068 kg (2352 lb).

Performance: Maximum speed, 125 mph. 0 to 60 mph, 8.6 sec. Fuel consumption, 28.0 mpg (at constant 75 mph).

Features: Slightly vague steering, but otherwise a pleasant car to drive, with wonderfully smooth engine behaviour. Well-equipped, with electric window lifts and removable glass sunroof.

MERCEDES-BENZ (D)   190E

Identity: Addition to Mercedes-Benz range with new body, slightly smaller than 200-Series, and ohc engine with inclined valves. Details below for injection version; carburettor model (190) also available.

Engine: Front-mounted four-cylinder with single ohc and electronic fuel injection. Engine mounted in-line. Bore, 89 mm, Stroke 80.3 mm; capacity 1,997 cc. Power, 122 bhp (90 kW) at 5,100 rpm; torque 129 lb ft (178 Nm) at 3,500 rpm.

Transmission: Rear-wheel drive; four-speed manual gearbox standard. Options are five-speed gearbox or four-speed automatic. Final drive ratio 3.23-to-1. Top gear mph at 1,000 rpm: 22.3.

Suspension: Front, independent, MacPherson struts; coil springs and gas-filled telescopic dampers. Anti-roll bar. Rear, independent, semi-trailing arms and anti-dive/anti-squat links; coil springs and gas-filled telescopic dampers. Anti-roll bar.

Steering: Recirculating ball, with varying ratio. Power assistance optional.

Brakes: Discs front and rear, servo-assisted.

Tyres: 175/70 R 14.

Dimensions: Length 4420 mm (174 in), width 1678 mm (66 in), height 1383 mm (54.4 in), wheelbase 2665 mm (105 in).

Unladen weight: 1080 kg (2380 lb).

Performance (Works): Maximum speed, 109 mph. 0 to 60 mph, 13.2 sec. Fuel consumption, 33.6 mpg (at constant 75 mph in fourth).

Features: Traditional Mercedes styling with familiar radiator grille surround and three-pointed star mascot, but immediate front recognition is shallower grille with only two horizontal stripes instead of three as on 200. Aerodynamic wheel plates. Neat finish.

MERCEDES-BENZ (D)   280TE

Identity: Top model in the Mercedes W123 estate car range. Body also available with four-cylinder engines of 2- or 2.3-litre capacity, or diesels of 2.4-litre and (five-cylinder) 3-litre. Very competent load carrier with large flat rear floor and huge back door.

Engine: Front-mounted six-cylinder with chain-driven twin ohc. Fuel injection and breakerless ignition. Bore, 86 mm, stroke 78.8 mm; capacity 2746 cc. Power, 185 bhp (138 kW) at 5800 rpm; torque 177 lb ft (245 Nm) at 4500 rpm.

Transmission: Rear-wheel drive; five-speed manual gearbox (to order), or four-speed automatic. Hypoid final drive, 3.58-to-1. Top gear mph at 1000 rpm: 24.8.

Suspension: Front, independent, wishbones and coil springs; telescopic dampers. Anti-roll bar. Rear, independent, semi-trailing arms; coil springs and telescopic dampers. Anti-roll bar. Hydraulic self-levelling, powered by engine.

Steering: Recirculating ball, power assisted.

Brakes: Discs front and rear, servo-assisted.

Tyres: 195/70 SR 14.

Dimensions: Length 4724 mm (186 in)), width 1784 mm (70.3 in), height 1425 mm (56 in), wheelbase 2794 mm (110 in).

Unladen weight: 1544 kg (3406 lb).

Performance (Works): Maximum speed, 124 mph. 0 to 60 mph, 10.8 sec. Fuel consumption, 19.1 mpg (at constant 75 mph).

Features: Roomy five-seater body and big load space. Roof fitted with longitudinal bars as standard, for which numerous purpose-built carriers are available. ABS anti-lock brakes optional.

MERCEDES-BENZ (D)   300SD Turbodiesel

Identity: Strangely, this model is not imported to Britain, although the standard 300D is available. Spacious and neatly appointed saloon with turbocharged five-cylinder diesel engine; four-door W123 body. America is chief market.

Engine: Front-mounted five-cylinder with single ohc, chain-driven. Cast iron head. Compression 21.5-to-1. Bore, 90.9 mm, stroke 92.4 mm; capacity 2998 cc. Power, 120 bhp (89.5 kW) at 4350 rpm; torque 167 lb ft (231 Nm) at 2400 rpm.

Transmission: Rear-wheel drive; four-speed automatic transmission standard (no manual version available). Top gear mph at 1000 rpm: 23.6.

Suspension: Front, independent, wishbones and coil springs; telescopic dampers. Anti-roll bar. Rear, independent, semi-trailing arms; coil springs and telescopic dampers. Anti-roll bar.

Steering: Recirculating ball, power assisted.

Brakes: Discs front and rear, servo-assisted.

Tyres: 195/70 HR 14.

Dimensions: Length 5145 mm (202.5 in for USA), width 1785 mm (70.3 in), height 1440 mm (56.7 in), wheelbase 2795 mm (110 in).

Unladen weight: 1445 kg (3186 lb).

Performance (Works): Maximum speed, 103 mph. Fuel consumption, 26.7 mpg (overall).

Features: Typically neat interior finish and quality of materials. Well-equipped and appealing to a higher market than the conventional diesel taxi versions with normally aspirated engines.

MERCEDES-BENZ (D)

380SEC

Identity: Not the top model in the Mercedes two-door coupé range but a very popular choice, giving remarkable combination of performance with comfort, space, style and even economy.

Engine: Front-mounted V8-cylinder with aluminium block and heads; two overhead camshafts; electronic ignition and injection. Bore, 88 mm, stroke 79 mm; capacity 3839 cc. Power, 204 bhp (152 kW) at 5250 rpm; torque 232 lb ft (321 Nm) at 3250 rpm.

Transmission: Rear-wheel drive; four-speed automatic by Daimler-Benz, with exceptionally high gearing for economy. Automatic kick-down to third right up to 110 mph! Top gear mph at 1000 rpm: 28.5.

Suspension: Front, independent, wishbones and coil springs, telescopic dampers; anti-roll bar. Rear, independent, semi-trailing arms, coil springs; telescopic dampers; anti-roll bar.

Steering: Recirculating ball with power assistance.

Brakes: Discs front and rear, servo-assisted, internally vented.

Tyres: 205/70 VR 14.

Dimensions: Length 4910 mm (193 in), width 1828 mm (72 in), height 1406 mm (55.4 in), wheelbase 2850 mm (112 in).

Unladen weight: 1592 kg (3507 lb).

Performance: Maximum speed, 131 mph. 0 to 60 mph, 9.1 sec. Fuel consumption, 26.2 mpg (at constant 75 mph).

Features: Lavish standard equipment including sunroof with electric control, electric window lifts and central locking; air conditioning extra. Anti-lock brakes also available.

MERCEDES-BENZ (D)   500SL

Identity: Original appearance of the Mercedes open two-seater sports with this body was in 1971, but this was the first car to be fitted with the new all-alloy V8, launched as the 500SL at Geneva 1980. Superbly refined and fast convertible.

Engine: Front-mounted V8-cylinder with chain-driven ohc each bank; alloy heads and block. Bosch K-Jetronic injection. Bore, 96.5 mm, stroke 85 mm; capacity 4973 cc. Power, 231 bhp (172 kW) at 4750 rpm; torque 298 lb ft (409 Nm) at 3200 rpm.

Transmission: Rear-wheel drive; Daimler-Benz four-speed automatic. Very high final drive ratio, 2.24-to-1. Limited slip diff. Top gear mph at 1000 rpm: 33.6.

Suspension: Front, independent, wishbones and coil springs; telescopic dampers. Anti-roll bar. Rear, independent, semi-trailing arms; coil springs and telescopic dampers. Anti-roll bar.

Steering: Recirculating ball, power assisted.

Brakes: Vented discs front, solid discs rear, servo-assisted.

Tyres: 205/70 VR 14.

Dimensions: Length 4389 mm (172.8 in), width 1790 mm (70.5 in), height 1300 mm (51.2 in), wheelbase 2455 mm (96.6 in).

Unladen weight: 1540kg (3395 lb).

Performance (Works): Maximum speed, 137 mph. 0 to 60 mph, 8.0 sec. Fuel consumption, 24.6 mpg (at constant 75 mph).

Features: Excellent sealing of hood and frameless glass side windows. Hood folds into a well, and is covered by rigid, hinged top. Hardtop available. Well finished and very fully equipped.

MERCEDES-BENZ (D)   300GD

Identity: New range of cross-country vehicles with the name *Geländewagen* (land car) launched 1979, and imported to Britain since end 1981. Choice of swb or lwb, and with three or five doors. Five-cylinder diesel engine or six-cylinder petrol.

Engine: Front-mounted five-cylinder with alloy head; single chain-driven ohc. Compression 21-to-1. Bore, 90.9 mm, stroke 92.4 mm; capacity 2998 cc. Power, 80 bhp (60 kW) at 4000 rpm; torque 127 lb ft (176 Nm) at 2400 rpm.

Transmission: Four-wheel drive; four-speed gearbox. Normal drive to rear wheels, plus front wheel drive selectable. Low ratio 4 wd available, and separate diff. locks for front and rear. Top gear mph at 1000 rpm: 17.3.

Suspension: Front, live axle on leading arms, with Panhard rod; coil springs and telescopic dampers. Rear, live axle on trailing arms, with Panhard rod; coil springs and telescopic dampers.

Steering: Recirculating ball, power assisted.

Brakes: Discs front, drums rear, servo-assisted.

Tyres: 6.50-16 XCL.

Dimensions: Length 4145 mm (163.2 in), width 1700 mm (66.9 in), height 1985 mm (78.1 in), wheelbase 2400 mm (94.5 in).

Unladen weight: 2082 kg (4585 lb).

Performance: Maximum speed, 82 mph. 0 to 60 mph, 23.7 sec. Fuel consumption, 19.3 mpg (overall).

Features: Very competent cross-country car. Lwb version length 4595 mm (181 in), wheelbase 2850 mm (112.2 in). Spare wheel on rear door. Six-cylinder model is 280GE, automatic transmission standard in Britain.

MERCURY (USA)

Capri RS

Identity: Two-door GT with opening hatchback. Standard engine is 2.3-litre 4-cyl., but options are the 3.8-litre V6 and 5.0-litre V8. Increased in power for 1983, the V8 is standard on the Capri RS. Other Capri versions are the L, GS and Black Magic.

Engine: Front-mounted V8-cylinder with four-choke carb. Central camshaft and pushrod ohv each bank. Bore, 101.6 mm, stroke 76 mm; capacity 4942 cc. Power (SAE): 177 bhp (133 kW) at 4200 rpm; torque 239 lb ft (330 Nm) at 2400 rpm.

Transmission: Rear-wheel drive; four-speed manual gearbox. Five-speed manual or three-speed automatic optional; automatic standard with 3.8-litre. Top gear mph at 1000 rpm: 32.3.

Suspension: Front, independent, MacPherson struts; coil springs and telescopic dampers. Anti-roll bar. Rear, live axle on trailing and transverse links; coil springs and telescopic dampers. Anti-roll bar optional.

Steering: Rack and pinion; power assistance optional.

Brakes: Vented discs front, drums rear, servo-assisted.

Tyres: 220/55 R 390 (with TR performance package).

Dimensions: Length 4549 mm (179.1 in), width 1755 mm (69.1 in), height 1318 mm (51.9 in), wheelbase 2550 mm (100.4 in).

Unladen weight: 1307 kg (2882 lb).

Performance (est.): Maximum speed, 120 mph. 0 to 60 mph, 6.9 sec. Fuel consumption, 17 mpg (overall).

Features: Four halogen headlamps. Opening rear hatch and folding rear seat. Options include opening roof panels (T-roof), leather-trimmed steering wheel, and TR performance package, including alloy wheels.

Identity: America's best-selling car, foreign or domestic, in 1982 was the Ford Escort, and the Lynx is a thinly disguised top alternative version under the Mercury banner. Almost the same car—two-door hatchback—is available in the American Ford range as the Escort GT.

Engine: Front-mounted four-cylinder with electronic fuel injection. Transverse installation. Belt-driven single ohc. Bore 80 mm, stroke 79.5 mm; capacity 1599 cc. Power (SAE): 80 bhp (60 kW) at 5800 rpm; torque 90 lb ft (125 Nm) at 3000 rpm.

Transmission: Front-wheel drive; five-speed manual gearbox. Three-speed automatic optional. Top gear mph at 1000 rpm: 24.9.

Suspension: Front, independent, MacPherson struts; coil springs and telescopic dampers. Anti-roll bar. Rear, independent, trailing arms and transverse arms; coil springs and telescopic dampers.

Steering: Rack and pinion, power assistance optional.

Brakes: Discs front, drums rear, servo-assisted.

Tyres: 165/80 R 13.

Dimensions: Length 4163 mm (163.9 in), width 1674 mm (65.9 in), height 1354 mm (53.3 in), wheelbase 2393 mm (94.2 in).

Unladen weight: 940 kg (2073 lb).

Performance (est.): Maximum speed, 105 mph. Fuel consumption, 28 mpg (overall).

Features: Spoilers front and rear. Fog lamps. Special door mirrors. Stone shields at lower edges of wings. Alloy wheels. Console and extra instruments.

Identity: Reintroduced as a new, six-seater capacity, mid-size car for 1983. Choice of 2.3-litre ohc engine, 3.3-litre in-line six, or 3.8-litre V6. The 2.3 is a four-cylinder and is also available for propane gas operation. 3.3-litre (details here) is standard for the estate car.

Engine: Front-mounted six-cylinder with side camshaft and pushrod ohv. Carter carburettor. In-line construction. Bore, 93.5 mm, stroke 79.4 mm; capacity 3273 cc. Power (SAE): 86 bhp (65 kW) at 3800 rpm; torque 151 lb ft (209 Nm) at 1400 rpm.

Transmission: Rear-wheel drive; four-speed manual gearbox. Three-speed automatic is optional for saloons, standard for estates. Top gear mph at 1000 rpm: 33.4.

Suspension: Front, independent, MacPherson struts and coil springs; Telescopic dampers. Anti-roll bar. Rear, live axle on trailing and semi-trailing links. Coil springs and telescopic dampers. Anti-roll bar optional.

Steering: Recirculating ball, power assisted.

Brakes: Vented discs front, drums rear, servo-assisted.

Tyres: 205/75 R 14.

Dimensions: Length 4991 mm (196.5 in), width 1803 mm (71 in), height 1361 mm (53.6 in), wheelbase 2680 mm (105.5 in).

Unladen weight: 1382 kg (3046 lb).

Performance (est.): Maximum speed, 98 mph. Fuel consumption, 20 mpg (at constant 75 mph).

Features: Split bench reclining seats, upholstered in cloth. Door trim panels with map pocket bins. Six-way power seat adjustment optional.

Identity: Three-door hatchback body as ordinary Metro, but black spoiler surround to back window, MG badge in centre of grille, and distinctive light alloy wheels.

Engine: Front-mounted four-cylinder with pushrod valve gear and single carb, transverse mounted; high compression and lively response. Bore, 70.6 mm, stroke 81.3 mm; capacity 1275 cc. Power, 72 bhp (54 kW) at 6000 rpm; torque 73 lb ft (101 Nm) at 4000 rpm.

Transmission: Front-wheel drive; four-speed gearbox located in engine sump. 7 in dia clutch, and 3.44-to-1 final drive. Top gear mph at 1000 rpm: 17.2.

Suspension: Front, independent, wishbones and BL Hydragas units; telescopic dampers; anti-roll bar. Rear, independent, Hydragas units, and dampers integral with springs.

Steering: Rack and pinion.

Brakes: Disc front, drums rear, servo-assisted.

Tyres: 155/70 SR 12.

Dimensions: Length 3404 mm (134 in), width 1547 mm (61 in), height 1359 mm (54 in), wheelbase 2250 mm (89 in).

Unladen weight: 811 kg (1786 lb).

Performance: Maximum speed, 100 mph. 0 to 60 mph, 12.2 sec. Fuel consumption, 39.1 mpg (at constant 75 mph).

Features: Successful attempt to bring traditional MG sporting character to a mundane family car. Rather harsh and noisy but a lot of fun to drive. Glass sunroof available.

MG (GB)   Metro Turbo

Identity: Performance version of Metro, introduced Birmingham 1982. Larger alloy wheels than standard MG Metro. Deep black spoiler with brake cooling inlets at front, and TURBO lettering on doors.

Engine: Front-mounted four-cylinder with pushrod ohv. Garrett AiResearch turbocharger; compression 9.4-to-1. Transverse installation. Bore, 70.6 mm, stroke 81.3 mm; capacity 1275 cc. Power, 93 bhp (70 kW) at 6130 rpm; torque 85 lb ft (118 Nm) at 2650 rpm.

Transmission: Front-wheel drive; four-speed manual gearbox in engine sump. Final drive ratio 3.21-to-1. Top gear mph at 1000 rpm: 18.6.

Suspension: Front, unequal length links; Hydragas springs and telescopic dampers. Anti-roll bar. Rear, independent, trailing arms; Hydragas springs with pre-loading by coil springs; internal damping in Hydragas unit. Transverse interconnection of Hydragas units. Anti-roll bar.

Steering: Rack and pinion.

Brakes: Vented discs front, drums rear, servo-assisted.

Tyres: 165/60 VR 13.

Dimensions: Length 3403 mm (134.1 in), width 1563 mm (61.6 in), height 1359 mm (53.5 in), wheelbase 2251 mm (88.6 in).

Unladen weight: 840 kg (1852 lb).

Performance (Works): Maximum speed, 112 mph. 0 to 60 mph. 9.9 sec. Fuel consumption, 35.1 mpg (at constant 75 mph).

Features: Exciting performance and tidy handling with taut suspension and very positive steering. LED boost gauge. Grey interior; sports front seats; one third split rear seat. Radio, rear wash/wipe, halogen headlamps and tinted glass standard.

Identity: Traditional sports car for real wind-in-the-hair fiends, with performance to match the looks, endowed by Rover engine. Hand-built two-seater with folding hood and detachable sidescreens.

Engine: Front-mounted V8-cylinder with alloy heads and block; hydraulic tappets. Twin Zenith-Stromberg carbs. Bore, 88.9 mm, stroke 71.1 mm; capacity 3528 cc. Power, 155 bhp (115.5 kW) at 5250 rpm; torque 193 lb ft (267 Nm) at 2500 rpm.

Transmission: Rear-wheel drive; five-speed gearbox with short travel change. Limited slip diff. Final drive hypoid bevel, 3.31-to-1. Top gear mph at 1000 rpm: 27.2.

Suspension: Front, independent, sliding pillars and coil springs; telescopic dampers. Rear, live axle on semi-elliptic leaf springs; lever arm dampers.

Steering: Worm and roller.

Brakes: Discs front, drums rear, servo-assisted.

Tyres: 205/60 VR 15.

Dimensions: Length 3740 mm (147-2 in), width 1575 mm (62 in), height 1320 mm (52 in), wheelbase 2490 mm (98 in).

Unladen weight: 830 kg (1830 lb).

Performance: Maximum speed, 123 mph. 0 to 60 mph, 6.5 sec. Fuel consumption, 20.5 mpg (overall).

Features: Short-travel and very harsh suspension gives some road-holding problems—a car you have to fight, picking a moment when all four wheels are on the ground; but lots of fun.

Identity: Undistinguished saloon derived from former Morris Marina, offering good value when size and space are related to price and equipment. Choice of 1.3- or 1.7-litre engine; also 2.0-litre, automatic only. Four-door saloon or five-door estate.

Engine: Front-mounted four-cylinder with single ohc; cylinders in-line, and engine positioned longitudinally. Bore, 84.5 mm, stroke 89 mm; capacity 1944 cc. Power, 90 bhp (67 kW) at 4750 rpm; torque 114 lb ft (158 Nm) at 3250 rpm.

Transmission: Rear-wheel drive; manual four-speed gearbox for 1.3- and 1.7-litre versions; 2.0 has automatic three-speed transmission standard. Top gear mph at 1000 rpm: 20.2

Suspension: Front, independent, wishbones and torsion bars, telescopic dampers; anti-roll bar. Rear, live axle on semi-elliptic leaf springs; telescopic dampers; anti-roll bar.

Steering: Rack and pinion.

Brakes: Discs front, drums rear, servo-assisted.

Tyres: 155 SR 13.

Dimensions: Length 4345 mm (171 in), width 1640 mm (64.5 in), height 1440 mm (56.7 in), wheelbase 2440 mm (96 in).

Unladen weight: 970 kg (2137 lb).

Performance: Maximum speed, 101 mph. 0 to 60 mph, 11.7 sec. Fuel consumption, 30.3 mpg (at constant 75 mph).

Features: Plain but functional; roomy and easy to drive. Good automatic with sensible control layout.

OLDSMOBILE (USA)

Cutlass Supreme Brougham

Identity: Choice of two-door coupé or four-door saloon, Supreme and Supreme Brougham. There are also the Calais two-door coupé, and Cruiser estate car. Standard engine is 3.8-litre V6; 4.3-litre V8 or 5.7-litre V8 diesel optional.

Engine: Front-mounted V6-cylinder with hydraulic tappets and electronic ignition. Twin-choke Rochester carb. Bore, 96.5 mm, stroke 86.4 mm; capacity 3791 cc. Power (SAE): 110 bhp (82 kW) at 3800 rpm; torque 190 lb ft (263 Nm) at 1600 rpm.

Transmission: Rear-wheel drive; Hydra-Matic automatic three-speed transmission; column-mounted change (centre change optional). Top gear mph at 1000 rpm: 30.4.

Suspension: Front, independent, wishbones and coil springs; telescopic dampers. Anti-roll bar. Rear, live axle on trailing arms, with upper links to diff; coil springs and telescopic dampers. Anti-roll bar optional.

Steering: Recirculating ball, power assisted.

Brakes: Vented discs front, drums rear, servo-assisted.

Tyres: 195/75 R 14.

Dimensions: Length 5080 mm (200 in), width 1819 mm (71.6 in), height 1438 mm (56.6 in), wheelbase 2746 mm (108.1 in).

Unladen weight: 1466 kg (3231 lb).

Performance (est.): Maximum speed, 98 mph. Fuel consumption, 18 mpg (overall).

Features: Squared-up and forward extended 'egg-crate' grille. Side and indicator lamps below bumper. Simulated convertible effect, but the Brougham is a fixed-head with dimunitive side window to rear of door each side.

OLDSMOBILE (USA)   Delta 88 Royale

Identity: There are four-door saloon or two-door coupé versions of the Delta Royale and Delta Brougham, plus the basic four-door Delta saloon. 3.8-litre V6 standard; two petrol V8s and V8 diesel optional.

Engine: Front-mounted V8-cylinder with central camshaft and push-rods. Four-choke Rochester carb. Bore, 96.5 mm, stroke 86 mm; capacity 5033 cc. Power (SAE): 140 bhp (104 kW) at 3600 rpm; torque 240 lb ft (332 Nm) at 1600 rpm.

Transmission: Rear-wheel drive; three-speed automatic standard. Optional automatic with overdrive. Top gear mph at 1000 rpm: 42.6 (overdrive version).

Suspension: Front, independent, wishbones and coil springs; telescopic dampers. Anti-roll bar. Rear, live axle on trailing links, with upper links to diff. Coil springs and telescopic dampers.

Steering: Recirculating ball, power assisted.

Brakes: Vented discs front, drums rear, servo-assisted.

Tyres: 205/75 R 15.

Dimensions: Length 5540 mm (218.1 in), width 1938 mm (76.3 in), height 1443 mm (56.8 in), wheelbase 2946 mm (116 in).

Unladen weight: 1603 kg (3534 lb).

Performance (est.): Maximum speed, 110 mph. Fuel consumption, 15 mpg (at constant 75 mph).

Features: Total range of eight models, as there are also three models coupé, saloon and Brougham—in the 98 range. Good equipment; big list of options.

OLDSMOBILE (USA)　　Toronado Brougham

Identity: Only one version of the huge Toronado is offered, with 4.1-litre V6 engine standard. Options are 5-litre V8 (see Delta 88), and 5.7-litre V8 diesel (detailed below).

Engine: Front-mounted V8-cylinder with central camshaft and push-rods. Compression ratio 21.6-to-1. Bore, 103.1 mm, stroke 86 mm; capacity 5737 cc. Power (SAE): 105 bhp (78 kW) at 3200 rpm; torque 200 lb ft (277 Nm) at 1600 rpm.

Transmission: Front-wheel drive; Hydra-Matic three-speed automatic plus overdrive standard. No manual option. Top gear mph at 1000 rpm; 40.0.

Suspension: Front, independent, wishbones and longitudinal torsion bars; telescopic dampers. Anti-roll bar. Rear, independent, semi-trailing arms, coil springs and telescopic dampers. Pneumatic self-levelling. Anti-roll bar.

Steering: Recirculating ball, power assisted.

Brakes: Vented discs front, drums rear, servo-assisted.

Tyres: 205/75 R 15.

Dimensions: Length 5232 mm (206 in), width 1814 mm (71.4 in), height 1400 mm (55.2 in), wheelbase 2896 mm (114 in).

Unladen weight: 1676 kg (3695 lb).

Performance (est.): Maximum speed, 90 mph. Fuel consumption, 18 mpg (overall).

Features: Six-way power seat with two memory positions. Simulated wire wheels. Two doors and separate luggage compartment; simulated convertible style. Rather wasteful of space and fuel, but no doubt imposing.

OPEL (E)

Identity: New GM small car, built in Spain with Austrian running gear. Choice of three engines (details here for top version). Vauxhall versions in Britain from 1983. Choice of saloon or (shorter) hatchback body. Three-box saloon version is Corsa TR.

Engine: Front-mounted four-cylinder with alloy head and toothed belt drive to ohc. Transverse mounting, with gearbox in line. Bore, 75 mm, stroke 73.4 mm; capacity 1297 cc. Power, 70 bhp (51 kW) at 5800 rpm; torque 73 lb ft (101 Nm) at 3800 rpm.

Transmission: Front-wheel drive; five-speed gearbox standard on this version (extra-cost option for other models). Final drive ratio 3.94-to-1. Top gear mph at 1000 rpm: 23.1.

Suspension: Front, independent, MacPherson struts; coil springs and telescopic dampers. Anti-roll bar. Rear, semi-independent, dead beam axle, trailing arms and coil springs. Telescopic dampers. Torsion beam axle gives anti-roll effects.

Steering: Rack and pinion.

Brakes: Discs front, drums rear, servo-assisted.

Tyres: 145 SR 13.

Dimensions: Length 3955 mm (156 in), width 1540 mm (60.6 in), height 1360 mm (53.5 in), wheelbase 2343 mm (92.2 in).

Unladen weight: 750 kg (1653 lb).

Performance (Works): Maximum speed, 100 mph. 0 to 60 mph, 13.5 sec. Fuel consumption, 44.8 mpg (at constant 75 mph).

Features: Quite well-equipped in Luxus form, with quartz clock, internally adjustable door mirror, and intermittent wipe, but no trip distance recorder, and boot is only self-locking.

OPEL (D)   Manta 1.8S Berlinetta

Identity: New version of familiar Manta, re-launched September 1982 with Vauxhall-Opel engine, designed for fwd installation, re-mounted in-line and with distributor repositioned at front. Drive to rear wheels. Engine capacity increased to 1796 cc, and five-speed gearbox standard. Choice of GT/J hatchback, or Berlinetta hatchback and two-door coupé.

Engine: Front-mounted four-cylinder with belt-driven single ohc; Varajet carb. Compression 9.2-to-1. Engine designed for high torque output. Bore, 84.8 mm, stroke 79.5 mm; capacity 1796 cc. Power, 90 bhp (67 kW) at 5400 rpm; torque 105.5 lb ft (146 Nm) at 3400 rpm.

Transmission: Rear-wheel drive; five-speed gearbox standard; three-speed GM automatic optional. Hypoid bevel final drive, ratio 3.47-to-1 (automatic 3.44). Top gear mph at 1000 rpm: 23.1.

Suspension: Front, independent, wishbones and coil springs; telescopic dampers. Anti-roll bar. Rear, dead beam axle with central joint, upper and lower arms; Panhard rod, telescopic dampers and coil springs. Anti-roll bar.

Steering: Rack and pinion.

Brakes: Discs front, drums rear, servo-assisted.

Tyres: 185/70 HR 13.

Dimensions: Length 4442 mm (174.9 in), width 1687 mm (66.4 in), height 1330 mm (52.4 in), wheelbase 2517 mm (99.1 in).

Unladen weight: Coupé, 1000 kg (2205 lb); Hatchback, 1025 kg (2260 lb).

Performance (Works): Maximum speed, 109 mph. 0 to 60 mph, 11.5 sec. Fuel consumption, 38.2 mpg (at constant 75 mph).

Features: Big improvement over previous model, now with more willing engine, higher gearing, better response and easier cruising at around 90 mph.

OPEL (D) Monza S 3.0E

Identity: Sleek, roomy two-door hatchback with long, sloping rear window. Very fast and extremely well-equipped. Numerous versions and equipment packages, but this one is the best of them all, with five-speed gearbox standard.

Engine: Front-mounted six-cylinder with cast iron head and block; chain-driven camshaft in head, working valves through hydraulic tappets. Bosch L-Jetronic injection. Bore, 95 mm, stroke 69.8 mm; capacity 2968 cc. Power, 180 bhp (134 kW) at 5800 rpm; torque 182 lb ft (252 Nm) at 4200 rpm.

Transmission: Rear-wheel drive; five-speed manual gearbox; three-speed automatic transmission (GM) optional. Top gear mph at 1000 rpm: 23.5.

Suspension: Front, independent, MacPherson struts, coil springs and telescopic dampers; anti-roll bar. Rear, independent, semi-trailing arms and mini-block coil springs; telescopic dampers. Anti-roll bar.

Steering: Recirculating ball, power assisted.

Brakes: Vented discs front, solid discs rear, servo-assisted.

Tyres: 205/60 VR 15.

Dimensions: Length 4758 mm (187 in), width 1734 mm (68.3 in), height 1334 mm (52.5 in), wheelbase 2668 mm (105 in).

Unladen weight: 1484 kg (3268 lb).

Performance: Maximum speed, 133 mph. 0 to 60 mph, 8.5 sec. Fuel consumption, 27.7 mpg (at constant 75 mph).

Features: Electric window lifts and sunroof; central locking (but not for tail hatch); headlamps wash/wipe. A magnificent and sadly under-rated car.

PANTHER (GB)   Kallista

Identity: Re-formed early 1981 from the original Panther Westwinds company, Panther Cars ended production of the Lima two-seater and replaced it with the rather similar Kallista, launched Birmingham 1982. Aluminium body with two-seater roadster style, and Ford running gear (XR3 engine, details follow, or 2.8-litre V6).

Engine: Front-mounted four-cylinder with alloy head and hemispherical combustion chambers. Belt-driven ohc. Compression ratio 9.5-to-1. Bore, 80 mm, stroke 79.5 mm; capacity 1597 cc. Power, 95 bhp (71 kW) at 6000 rpm; torque 98lb ft (136 Nm) at 4000 rpm.

Transmission: Rear-wheel drive; four-speed manual gearbox standard (five-speed optional). Automatic available with 2.8-litre engine. Final drive ratio 3.75-to-1. Top gear mph at 1000 rpm: 22.0 (fifth); 18.0 (fourth).

Suspension: Front, independent, wishbones and coil springs; telescopic dampers. Rear, live axle on trailing links, with Panhard rod; coil springs and telescopic dampers.

Steering: Rack and pinion.

Brakes: Discs front, drums rear, servo-assisted.

Tyres: 165 SR 13 (185/70 HR 13 optional).

Dimensions: Length 3905 mm (153.7 in), width 1712 mm (67.4 in), height 1245 mm (49 in), wheelbase 2549 mm (100.3 in).

Unladen weight: 870 kg (1918 lb).

Performance (Works): Maximum speed, 105 mph. 0 to 60 mph, 8.5 sec. Fuel consumption, 35 mpg (overall, estimated).

Features: Two-seater with detachable hood and wind-up side windows. Fairly basic standard equipment but long list of options.

PEUGEOT (F)

Identity: Abbreviated three-door hatchback; also available are the 104Z and the coupé ZA with smaller engines (1124 and 954 cc). ZS has 1360 cc engine, and at Paris 1982 this additional more powerful version (detailed below) was announced; 72 bhp ZS continues, in addition.

Engine: Front-mounted four-cylinder with alloy head and chain-driven ohc. Engine transverse, and inclined rearward at 72 deg. Bore, 75 mm, stroke 77 mm; capacity 1360 cc. Power, 76 bhp (57 kW) at 5800 rpm; torque 79 lb ft (109 Nm) at 2800 rpm.

Transmission: Front-wheel drive; five-speed manual gearbox in line with engine. Top gear mph at 1000 rpm: 18.5.

Suspension: Front, independent, MacPherson struts; coil springs and telescopic dampers. Anti-roll bar. Rear, independent, trailing arms and coil springs; telescopic dampers. Anti-roll bar.

Steering: Rack and pinion.

Brakes: Discs front, drums rear, servo-assisted.

Tyres: 165/70 SR 13.

Dimensions: Length 3366 mm (132.5 in), width 1522 mm (60 in), height 1359 mm (53.5 in), wheelbase 2230 mm (87.8 in).

Unladen weight: 810 kg (1786 lb).

Performance (Works): Maximum speed, 102 mph. 0 to 60 mph, 11.6 sec. Fuel consumption, 35.8 mpg (at constant 75 mph).

Features: Halogen headlamps. Crisp handling and accurate steering. Handy little car with good performance in this latest version.

Identity: Extraordinary, the things that have been done to the Peugeot 504 over the years since its 1973 introduction, culminating in this four-wheel drive conversion by Dangel, launched Paris 1982. Choice of 1971 cc petrol or (details follow) 2304 cc. diesel.

Engine: Front-mounted four-cylinder installed in line and inclined to the right at 20 deg. Compression 22.2-to-1. Bore, 94 mm, stroke 83 mm; capacity 2304 cc. Power, 70 bhp (50.5 kW) at 4500 rpm; torque 93.3 lb ft (129 Nm) at 2000 rpm.

Transmission: Four-wheel drive; four-speed manual gearbox. Constant rear drive, selectable front drive. Low ratio transfer gearbox. Limited slip diff front and rear. Top gear mph at 1000 rpm: 17.9

Suspension: Front, live axle, MacPherson struts; coil springs and telescopic dampers. Anti-roll bar. Suspension strengthened. Rear, live axle, torque tube, trailing arms and Panhard rod; twin coil springs each side; telescopic dampers. Anti-roll bar. Suspension strengthened.

Steering: Rack and pinion.

Brakes: Discs front, drums rear, servo-assisted.

Tyres: 185-16 XCM.

Dimensions: Length 4805 mm (189 in), width 1695 mm (66.7 in), height 1555 mm (61.2 in), wheelbase 2900 mm (114 in).

Unladen weight: 1480 kg (3262 lb).

Performance (Estimated): Maximum speed, 80 mph. 0 to 60 mph, 23 sec. Fuel consumption, 28.2 mpg (at constant 75 mph).

Features: Chassis reinforced, and larger front disc brakes fitted. Suspension modifications to give higher ground clearance. Conversion available for Pick-up, Estate Car, or saloon.

PEUGEOT (F)   505 GR Estate car

Identity: Spacious load carrier with very sensible body, and huge rear tailgate; uncluttered load area. Available as estate, or as the family model, with three rows of seats. Choice of 1971 cc petrol or 2498 cc diesel; estate can also have less powerful engine, with same capacity but single-choke carb.

Engine: Front-mounted four-cylinder with alloy head, and cast iron block with dry liners. Compression 8.8-to-1. Pushrod ohv. Bore, 88 mm, stroke 81 mm; capacity 1971 cc. Power, 96 bhp (72 kW) at 5200 rpm; torque 116 lb ft (160 Nm) at 3000 rpm.

Transmission: Rear-wheel drive; four-speed gearbox; hypoid bevel final drive, ratio 3.89-to-1, Estate GR and petrol-engined family models are available with three-speed automatic. Top gear mph at 1000 rpm: 18.9.

Suspension: Front, independent, MacPherson struts, coil springs and telescopic dampers. Anti-roll bar. Rear, Live axle on trailing arms; coil springs and telescopic dampers. Anti-roll bar.

Steering: Rack and pinion, power assistance standard.

Brakes: Discs front, drums rear, servo-assisted.

Tyres: 175 HR 14.

Dimensions: Length 4898 mm (192 in), width 1730 mm (68 in), height 1540 mm (60.6 in), wheelbase 2900 mm (114.2 in).

Unladen weight: 1274 kg (2803 lb).

Performance: Maximum speed, 98 mph. 0 to 60 mph, 12.4 sec. Fuel consumption, 28.5 mpg (at constant 75 mph).

Features: Neatly finished and built, and very comfortable seats and ride. Spare wheel carried in open tray under back floor. Huge flat floor space when rear seat is tipped forward.

PLYMOUTH (USA)　　　　Reliant Estate Car

Identity: Medium-size estate car with five- or occasional six-seater capacity, and front drive. Other bodies include four-door saloon, and Custom two-door coupé with diminutive vertical window to rear of door each side. Four-cyl 2.2- or 2.6-litre engine.

Engine: Front-mounted four-cylinder with belt-driven ohc and hydraulic tappets. Alloy head. Transverse installation. Bore, 87.5 mm, stroke 92 mm; capacity 2213 cc. Power, 84 bhp (62.5 kW) at 4800 rpm; torque 109 lb ft (151 Nm) at 2400 rpm.

Transmission: Front-wheel drive; four-speed manual gearbox. Five-speed gearbox or three-speed automatic transmission optional. Top gear mph at 1000 rpm: 28.3.

Suspension: Front, independent, MacPherson struts; coil springs and telescopic dampers. Anti-roll bar. Rear, dead beam axle on trailing arms, with Panhard rod. Coil springs and telescopic dampers. Anti-roll bar.

Steering: Rack and pinion, power assistance optional.

Brakes: Vented discs front, drums rear, servo-assisted.

Tyres: 185/70 R 13.

Dimensions: Length 4475 mm (176.2 in), width 1646 mm (57.6 in), height 1331 mm (52.4 in), wheelbase 2543 mm (100.1 in).

Unladen weight: 1127 kg (2484 lb).

Performance (est.): Maximum speed, 95 mph. Fuel consumption, 24 mpg (overall).

Features: Quite comfortable ride, and reasonably responsive controls. Good compromise of internal space without excessive external bulk. Reasonably well-equipped, and good choice of extras.

PONTIAC (USA)

Firebird Trans Am

Identity: Fascinating contradiction of the European popular concept of the American car. Two doors, 2+2 accommodation, and opening rear hatch. Three models (others are standard Firebird and S/E), and wide choice of engines starting with 2.5-litre 4-cyl.

Engine: Front-mounted V8-cylinder with electronic fuel injection. Compression 8.6-to-1. Bore, 94.9 mm, stroke 88.4 mm; capacity 5004 cc. Power (SAE): 165 bhp (123 kW) at 4200 rpm; torque 240 lb ft (332 Nm) at 2400 rpm.

Transmission: Rear-wheel drive; four-speed manual gearbox. Three-speed automatic transmission available. Top gear mph at 1000 rpm: 23.2.

Suspension: Front, independent, modified MacPherson struts, with coil spring separate from strut. Anti-roll bar. Rear, live axle on trailing arms, with upper links to diff. Coil springs and telescopic dampers. Anti-roll bar optional.

Steering: Recirculating ball, power assisted.

Brakes: Discs front, and (optional) rear, servo-assisted.

Tyres: 215/65 SR 15.

Dimensions: Length 4835 mm (190.3 in), width 1840 mm (72.4 in), height 126.5 mm (49.8 in), wheelbase 2565 mm (101 in).

Unladen weight: 1415 kg (3120 lb).

Performance (est.): Maximum speed, 120 mph. Fuel consumption, 17 mpg (overall).

Features: Reclining bucket seats in cloth or vinyl. Electric rear hatch release. Pop-up headlamps. Wing-type rear spoiler in black identifies Trans Am (body colour spoiler on S/E).

PONTIAC (USA)   Grand Prix Brougham

Identity: Top model of the Pontiac Bonneville range, for which there are saloon and estate car models with 3.8-litre V6 standard. Grand Prix comes as two-door saloon, with two trim levels for Brougham special edition, or as the luxury Brougham Landau. Engine options are 4.1-litre V6 or 5.7-litre V8 diesel.

Engine: Front-mounted V6-cylinder with hydraulic tappets. Twin-choke Rochester carb. Electronic ignition. Bore, 96.5 mm, stroke 86.4 mm; capacity 3791 cc. Power (SAE): 111 bhp (83 kW) at 3800 rpm; torque 357 lb ft (258 Nm) at 1600 rpm.

Transmission: Rear-wheel drive; Hydra-Matic automatic transmission standard. Column-mounted selector. Final drive 2.41-to-1. Top gear mph at 1000 rpm: 30.5.

Suspension: Front, independent, wishbones and coil springs; telescopic dampers. Anti-roll bar. Rear, live axle on trailing arms; upper links on to diff. Coil springs and telescopic dampers. Anti-roll bar optional.

Steering: Recirculating ball, power assisted.

Brakes: Vented discs front, drums rear, servo-assisted.

Tyres: 195/75 R 14.

Dimensions: Length 5128 mm (201.9 in), width 1831 mm (72.1 in), height 1389 mm (54.7 in), wheelbase 2746 mm (108.1 in).

Unladen weight: 1535 kg (3383 lb).

Performance (est.): Maximum speed, 95 mph. Fuel consumption, 18 mpg (at constant 75mph).

Features: Ball joint wear indicators on front suspension lower arms. Luxury furnishings; folding rear seat, split 60/40.

PONTIAC (USA)

Identity: Based on the GM X-car, the 6000 is completely different inside. Standard or LE trim, and choice of four-door saloon or two-door coupé. Fuel-injected 2.5-litre engine is basic power unit; options are 2.8-litre V6, or 4.3-litre diesel V6.

Engine: Front-mounted four-cylinder with hydraulic tappets and electronic injection and ignition. Transverse installation. Bore, 101.6 mm, stroke 76.2 mm; capacity 2471 cc. Power (SAE): 90 bhp (67 kW) at 4000 rpm; torque 132 lb ft (182 Nm) at 2400 rpm.

Transmission: Front-wheel drive; automatic three-speed transmission with column-mounted control. No manual option. Top gear mph at 1000 rpm: 24.9.

Suspension: Front, independent, MacPherson struts; coil springs and telescopic dampers. Anti-roll bar. Rear, dead torsion beam axle with longitudinal links, and Panhard rod; coil springs and telescopic dampers. Optional electronic self-levelling.

Steering: Rack and pinion, servo assisted.

Brakes: Vented discs front, drums rear, servo-assisted.

Tyres: 185/80 R 13.

Dimensions: Length 4806 mm (189.2 in), width 1720 mm (67.7 in), height 1367 mm (53.8 in), wheelbase 2665 mm (104.9 in).

Unladen weight: 1219 kg (2687 lb).

Performance (est.): Maximum speed, 95 mph. Fuel consumption, 24 mpg (overall).

Features: Electric window lifts optional. Large boot due to high rear deck line. Air conditioning and electric door mirrors optional.

PORSCHE (D)

Identity: One of the few cars with an air-cooled rear engine is the Porsche 911, and this is the exciting turbocharged version giving phenomenal performance. Big spoiler wing at rear is an identifying feature.

Engine: Rear-mounted six-cylinder with horizontally opposed layout. Air-cooled, Bosch K-Jetronic fuel injection, and KKK turbocharger. Single ohc each bank (chain). Bore, 97 mm, stroke 74.4 mm; capacity 3299 cc. Power, 300 bhp (221 kW) at 5500 rpm; torque 303 lb ft (412 Nm) at 4000 rpm.

Transmission: Rear-wheel drive; five-speed manual gearbox. No automatic version. Limited slip diff. Top gear mph at 1000 rpm: 26.4.

Suspension: Front, independent, MacPherson struts; torsion bars and telescopic dampers. Anti-roll bar. Rear, independent semi-trailing arms; torsion bars and telescopic dampers. Anti-roll bar.

Steering: Rack and pinion.

Brakes: Vented discs front and rear, servo-assisted.

Tyres: 185/70 VR 15 (front); 215/60 VR 15 (rear).

Dimensions: Length 4291 mm (168.9 in), width 1652 mm (65 in), height 1320 mm (52 in), wheelbase 2273 mm (89.5 in).

Unladen weight: 1160 kg (2557 lb).

Performance: Maximum speed, 153 mph. 0 to 60 mph, 6.1 sec. Fuel consumption, 18.5 mpg (at constant 75 mph).

Features: Terrific response when the turbo comes into effect; slight lag, but not excessive. Some deficiencies due to air cooling—noisy, and heating difficult to control—but still exciting.

Identity: One of the world's finest grand touring cars, with tremendous care given to roadholding. Transaxle arrangement (gearbox at rear) to ensure optimum weight distribution. S version has more powerful engine, and is distinguished by wind deflectors for front wheels and rear spoiler.

Engine: Front-mounted V8-cylinder with all-alloy construction. Single belt-driven ohc each bank. Hydraulic tappets. Bore, 97 mm, stroke 79 mm; capacity 4664 cc. Power, 300 bhp (221 kW) at 5900 rpm; torque 283 lb ft (385 Nm) at 4500 rpm.

Transmission: Rear-wheel drive; five-speed manual gearbox in transaxle. Three-speed automatic optional. Top gear mph at 1000 rpm: 25.6.

Suspension: Front, independent, wishbones, coaxial coil springs and telescopic dampers. Anti-roll bar. Rear, independent, semi-trailing arms with self-compensating wheel alignment control in severe cornering (Weissach axle). Coil springs and telescopic dampers. Anti-roll bar.

Steering: Rack and pinion, power assisted.

Brakes: Vented discs front and rear, servo-assisted.

Tyres: 225/50 VR 16.

Dimensions: Length 4448 mm (175.1 in), width 1836 mm (72.3 in), height 313 mm (51.7 in), wheelbase 2499 mm (98.4 in).

Unladen weight: 1450 kg (3197 lb).

Performance: Maximum speed, 152 mph. 0 to 60 mph, 6.7 sec. Fuel consumption, 22.4 mpg (at constant 75 mph).

Features: Inclined headlamps, tip forward for use. Pressure jet headlamp washers. Aerodynamic body with energy-absorbing front and tail instead of separate bumpers. Folding separate rear seats.

Identity: New in Germany in mid-1981, high-performance derivative of 924, with Porsche's own new 2½-litre four-cyl engine. Body basically the same, but note the enlarged wheel arches and deep front spoiler. Exciting, and in the real Porsche mould.

Engine: Front-mounted four-cylinder with alloy block and head, linerless block. Breakerless ignition; Bosch L Jetronic fuel injection. Bore, 100 mm, stroke 78.9 mm; capacity 2479 cc. Power, 163 bhp (122 kW) at 5800 rpm; torque 151 lb ft (209 Nm) at 3000 rpm.

Transmission: Rear-wheel drive; five-speed manual gearbox; three-speed automatic transmission optional. Top gear mph at 1000 rpm: 22.8.

Suspension: Front, independent, MacPherson struts; coil springs and telescopic dampers. Anti-roll bar. Rear, independent, semi-trailing arms and torsion bars; telescopic dampers. Anti-roll bar.

Steering: Rack and pinion.

Brakes: Vented discs front and rear, servo-assisted.

Tyres: 215/60 VR 15.

Dimensions: Length 4200 mm (165.3 in), width 1735 mm (68.3 in), height 1275 mm (50 in), wheelbase 2400 mm (94.5 in).

Unladen weight: 1195 kg (2632 lb).

Performance: Maximum speed, 137 mph. 0 to 60 mph, 7.4 sec. Fuel consumption, 30.1 mpg (at constant 75 mph).

Features: As for 924, gearbox is at rear in transaxle, with torque tube for prop shaft of small diameter. Four high-back seats, minimal rear legroom; opening rear window.

RANGE ROVER (GB)　　In Vogue Automatic

Identity: Important 1982 addition to Range Rover choice was automatic version; special In Vogue limited edition launched at same time, with luxury interior furnishings. Mechanically otherwise much the same, with permanent four-wheel drive and V8 alloy engine.

Engine: Front-mounted V8-cylinder with alloy heads and block; ohv, hydraulic tappets; twin Zenith-Stromberg carbs. Compression 9.35-to-1. Bore, 88.9 mm, stroke 71.1 mm; capacity 3528 cc. Power, 125 bhp (93 kW) at 4000 rpm; torque 190 lb ft (263 Nm) at 2500 rpm.

Transmission: Four-wheel drive; diffs. front, rear and centre. Centre diff. lockable for severe conditions. Chrysler A727 three-speed automatic transmission. Top gear mph at 1000 rpm: 23.7.

Suspension: Front, live axle on radius arms and Panhard rod; long travel coil springs; telescopic dampers. Rear, live axle on radius arms and Panhard rod; coil springs; telescopic dampers with self-levelling strut.

Steering: Recirculating ball, power assisted.

Brakes: Discs front, and rear, servo-assisted.

Tyres: 205 R 16.

Dimensions: Length 4470 mm (176 in), width 1718 mm (67.7 in), height 1778 mm (70 in), wheelbase 2591 mm (102 in).

Unladen weight: 1892 kg (4163 lb).

Performance (Works): Maximum speed, 96 mph. 0 to 60 mph, 16.7 sec. Fuel consumption, 16.2 mpg (overall).

Features: Generously trimmed inside for cross-country vehicle, with such refinements as wood fillets on doors and pile carpet; but all materials are of durable type, and carpets readily removable.

Identity: Unusual semi-utility car, produced initially for Barbados; added to British market from January 1983. Galvanised steel box section chassis. Glass fibre body with sliding side windows and removable canvas tilt.

Engine: Front-mounted four-cylinder with all-alloy construction. Pushrod ohv. Compression 9.5-to-1. Bore, 62.5 mm, stroke 69.1 mm; capacity 848 cc. Power, 40 bhp (30 kW) at 5500 rpm; torque 45 lb ft (62 Nm) at 3500 rpm.

Transmission: Rear-wheel drive; four-speed manual gearbox. Reliant semi-floating final drive, ratio 4.1-to-1. Top gear mph at 1000 rpm: 17.0.

Suspension: Front, independent, wishbones and coil springs; telescopic dampers. Anti-roll bar. Rear, live axle on semi-elliptic leaf springs. Telescopic dampers.

Steering: Rack and pinion.

Brakes: Drums front and rear.

Tyres: 155 SR 12.

Dimensions: Length 3380 mm (133 in), width 1540 mm (60.7 in), height 1520 mm (59.9 in), wheelbase 2146 mm (84.5 in).

Unladen weight: 563 kg (1241 lb).

Performance (est.): Maximum speed, 75 mph. Fuel consumption, no data available.

Features: Removable tail gate. Several options, including detachable hardtop of glass fibre. Transparent side panels in hood, and fitted rear seat, also options.

RELIANT (GB)   Scimitar GTC

Identity: Small-production convertible four-seater with glass fibre body on galvanised steel chassis. Hood folds down into a well behind back seat, leaving fixed roll bar in position. Ford Cologne 2.8-litre engine.

Engine: Front-mounted V6-cylinder with pushrod ohv. Weber carb. Bore, 93 mm, stroke 68.5 mm; capacity 2792 cc. Power, 135 bhp (101 kW) at 5200 rpm; torque 159 lb ft (220 Nm) at 3000 rpm.

Transmission: Rear-wheel drive; four-speed manual gearbox plus overdrive operating on third and fourth. Three-speed automatic optional. Top gear mph at 1000 rpm: 26.7.

Suspension: Front, independent, wishbones and coil springs; telescopic dampers. Anti-roll bar. Rear, live axle on trailing arms with Watts linkage; coil springs and telescopic dampers.

Steering: Rack and pinion; power assistance optional.

Brakes: Discs front, drums rear, servo-assisted.

Tyres: 185 HR 14.

Dimensions: Length 4432 mm (174.5 in), width 1720 mm (67.8 in), height 1321 mm (52 in), wheelbase 2637 mm (103.8 in).

Unladen weight: 1266 kg (2790 lb).

Performance: Maximum speed, 119 mph. 0 to 60 mph, 10.0 sec. Fuel consumption, 29.4 mpg (at constant 75 mph).

Features: Overdrive standard unless automatic transmission is specified. Long-legged fast cruising car with the unusual appeal of a fully convertible four-seater.

RENAULT (F)　　　　　　　　　5 Gordini Turbo

Identity: Derived from Renault's motor sport experience with turbo-charging, high performance version of the 5 intended to give vigorous road performance with good economy.

Engine: Front-mounted four-cylinder in-line, longitudinally mounted, with transmission ahead of engine, and Garrett turbocharger. Bore, 76 mm, stroke 77 mm; capacity 1397 cc. Power, 110 bhp (82 kW) at 6000 rpm; torque 109 lb ft (151 Nm) at 4000 rpm.

Transmission: Front-wheel drive; five-speed gearbox standard with all gears indirect; 7.5 in dia clutch. Top gear mph at 1000 rpm: 19.1.

Suspension: Front, independent, wishbones and torsion bars; telescopic dampers; anti-roll bar. Rear, independent, trailing arms and torsion bars; telescopic dampers; anti-roll bar. Torsion bars overlap: longer wheelbase left side.

Steering: Rack and pinion.

Brakes: Discs front, and rear, servo-assisted.

Tyres: 155/70 HR 13.

Dimensions: Length 3555 mm (140 in), width 1525 mm (60 in), height 1400 mm (55.5 in), wheelbase 2412/2442 mm (95/96¼ in).

Unladen weight: 850 kg (1877 lb).

Performance: Maximum speed, 113 mph. 0 to 60 mph, 9.8 sec. Fuel consumption, 33.2 mpg (at constant 75 mph).

Features: Impressive blend of performance and lively, sporting handling, and potential for good economy in relation to speed. Alloy wheels standard. Turbo badge on back.

RENAULT (F) 9GTL

Identity: Simple three-box saloon with thoroughly sound design and ingenious multi-way seat adjustment. Launched Frankfurt 1981, in Britain March 1982. Range of trim packs and choice of three engines, of which GTL is the most economical. Single automatic model also available.

Engine: Front-mounted four-cylinder with alloy head on cast iron block. Pushrod ohv. Breakerless ignition. Transverse installation. Bore, 76 mm, stroke 77 mm; capacity 1397 cc. Power, 60 bhp (45 kW) at 5250 rpm; torque 74 lb ft (102 Nm) at 3000 rpm.

Transmission: Front-wheel drive; five-speed manual gearbox. Helical spur final drive, ratio 4.21-to-1. Top gear mph at 1000 rpm: 20.5.

Suspension: Front, independent, MacPherson struts, coil springs and telescopic dampers. Anti-roll bar. Rear, independent, trailing arms and transverse torsion bars. Telescopic dampers. Anti-roll bar.

Steering: Rack and pinion.

Brakes: Discs front, drums rear, servo-assisted.

Tyres: 155S SR 13.

Dimensions: Length 4063 mm (160 in), width 1634 mm (64.3 in), height 1330 mm (52.4 in), wheelbase 2477 mm (97.5 in).

Unladen weight: 802 kg (1768 lb).

Performance: Maximum speed, 94 mph (fourth). 0 to 60 mph, 14.2 sec. Fuel consumption, 38.7 mpg (at constant 75 mph).

Features: Impressive fuel economy. Centre console, and comprehensive instrumentation with multiple warning tell-tales but no rev counter.

RENAULT (F)   Fuego GTX

Identity: Stylish coupé, two-door four-seater hatchback. Range of trim packs and engines, starting with 1397 cc unit. GTX is top version, with 2-litre engine. Third engine option is the 1647 cc unit.

Engine: Front-mounted four-cylinder with single belt-driven ohc. Alloy head and block. Weber carb. Bore, 88 mm, stroke 82 mm; capacity 1995 cc. Power, 110 bhp (83 kW) at 5500 rpm; torque 120 lb ft (166 Nm) at 3000 rpm.

Transmission: Front-wheel drive; five-speed manual gearbox. Three-speed automatic optional. Final drive ratio 3.78-to-1 (automatic 3.56). Top gear mph at 1000 rpm: 20.8.

Suspension: Front, independent, wishbones and coil springs, telescopic dampers. Anti-roll bar. Rear, dead beam axle on longitudinal links and central triangular link; coil springs and telescopic dampers. Anti-roll bar.

Steering: Rack and pinion.

Brakes: Vented discs front, solid discs rear, servo-assisted.

Tyres: 175/70 SR 13.

Dimensions: Length 4359 mm (171.6 in), width 1692 mm (66.6 in), height 1316 mm (51.8 in), wheelbase 2438 mm (96 in).

Unladen weight: 1170 kg (2580 lb).

Performance: Maximum speed, 113 mph. 0 to 60 mph, 10.0 sec. Fuel consumption, 34.5 mpg (at constant 75 mph).

Features: Pleasing combination of sporting characteristics, good performance, and impressive comfort. High-back seats. Alloy wheels. Well-equipped, including electric window lifts.

Identity: Top model of Renault range, with fuel injection version of PRV (Peugeot-Renault-Volvo) conjoint V6 engine, and lavish standard equipment. Four-door hatchback body. Four round headlamps and distinctive alloy wheels are identifying features.

Engine: Front-mounted V6-cylinder with alloy heads and block, and chain-driven ohc each bank. Bosch K-Jetronic injection. Bore, 88 mm, stroke 73 mm; capacity 2664 cc. Power, 140 bhp (104.5 kW) at 5500 rpm; torque 161 lb ft (223 Nm) at 3000 rpm.

Transmission: Front-wheel drive; five-speed manual gearbox. Three-speed automatic optional. Top gear mph at 1000 rpm: 22.6.

Suspension: Front, independent, wishbones and coil springs; telescopic dampers. Anti-roll bar. Rear, independent, longitudinal links and transverse links; coil springs and telescopic dampers. Anti-roll bar.

Steering: Rack and pinion, power assisted.

Brakes: Vented discs front, solid discs rear, servo-assisted.

Tyres: 175 HR 14.

Dimensions: Length 4521 mm (178 in), width 1727 mm (68 in), height 1422 mm (56 in), wheelbase 2667 mm (105 in).

Unladen weight: 1340 kg (2954 lb).

Performance: Maximum speed, 115 mph. 0 to 60 mph, 10.3 sec. Fuel consumption, 19.0 mpg (at constant 75 mph).

Features: Very comfortable ride, and quiet, vigorous performance. Electric sunroof, central locking, headlamps wash/wipe, electric tailgate and fuel filler flap release, all standard in Britain.

Identity: Other than the giant Phantom VI limousine, built only to order, the Camargue is by a long way the most expensive Rolls-Royce. Two-door four-seater saloon body styled by Pininfarina. Very wide look at front; tapering rear shoulders.

Engine: Front-mounted V8-cylinder with alloy block and heads; hydraulic tappets. Single Solex carb. Compression 9.0-to-1. Bore, 104.1 mm, stroke 99.1 mm; capacity 6750 cc. Power and torque—no data disclosed by Rolls-Royce.

Transmission: Rear-wheel drive; GM 400 automatic transmission standard, with Rolls-Royce electric selector on steering column. Top gear mph at 1000 rpm: 26.3.

Suspension: Front, independent, wishbones and coil springs; telescopic dampers. Anti-roll bar. Rear, independent, trailing arms, coil springs and hydro-pneumatic auxiliary springs, with self-levelling provision. Telescopic dampers; anti-roll bar.

Steering: Rack and pinion, power assisted.

Brakes: Vented discs front, solid discs rear, servo-assisted (pressure hydraulic system).

Tyres: 235/70 HR 15.

Dimensions: Length 5170 mm (203.5 in), width 1920 mm (75.6 in), height 1470 mm (57.9 in), wheelbase 3050 mm (120.1 in).

Unladen weight: 2330 kg (5135 lb).

Performance (Works): Maximum speed, 118 mph. Fuel consumption, 14.6 mpg (at constant 75 mph).

Features: Equipment largely as Silver Spirit and Corniche, including elaborate bi-level air conditioning system. Extra cost mainly goes into the special hand-built body.

ROLLS-ROYCE (GB)   Corniche convertible

Identity: Although similar to the now-discontinued Silver Shadow, the Corniche has all the suspension revisions of the later Spirit, and was in fact up-dated in this respect before Silver Spirit was introduced.

Engine: Front-mounted V8-cylinder with alloy block and heads; hydraulic tappets. Single Solex carb. Compression 9.0-to-1. Bore, 104.1 mm, stroke 99.1 mm; capacity 6750 cc. Power and torque—no data disclosed by Rolls-Royce.

Transmission: Rear-wheel drive; GM 400 automatic transmission standard, with Rolls-Royce electric selector on steering column. Top gear mph at 1000 rpm: 26.3.

Suspension: Front, independent, wishbones and coil springs; telescopic dampers. Anti-roll bar. Rear, independent, trailing arms, coil springs, and hydro-pneumatic auxiliary springs, with self-levelling provision. Telescopic dampers; anti-roll bar.

Steering: Rack and pinion, power assisted.

Brakes: Vented discs front, solid discs rear, servo-assisted (pressure hydraulic system).

Tyres: 235/70 HR 15.

Dimensions: Length 5194 mm (204.5 in), width 1829 mm (72 in), height 1519 mm (59.8 in), wheelbase 3050 mm (120.1 in).

Unladen weight: 2359 kg (5200 lb).

Performance: Maximum speed, 126 mph. 0 to 60 mph, 9.7 sec. Fuel consumption, 14.6 mpg (at constant 75 mph).

Features: Hood folds easily down, but tonneau cover is fiddly to install. Magnificent motoring with hood down, at least for those in front; rather breezy in rear. Beautifully appointed.

ROLLS-ROYCE (GB)   Silver Spur

Identity: Cheapest available Rolls-Royce is Silver Spirit, with similar body to Bentley Mulsanne except for radiator surround (see Mulsanne Turbo). Silver Spur is mechanically similar, but has longer wheelbase and is available with division.

Engine: Front-mounted V8-cylinder with alloy block and heads; hydraulic tappets. Twin SU carbs. Compression 9.0-to-1. Bore, 104.1 mm, stroke 99.1 mm; capacity 6750 cc. Power and torque—no data disclosed by Rolls-Royce.

Transmission: Rear-wheel drive; GM 400 automatic transmission standard, with Rolls-Royce modifications and electric column control. Top gear mph at 1000 rpm: 26.3.

Suspension: Front, independent, wishbones and coil springs; telescopic dampers. Anti-roll bar. Rear, independent, trailing arms, coil springs, and hydro-pneumatic auxiliary springs, with self-levelling provision. Telescopic dampers; anti-roll bar.

Steering: Rack and pinion, power assisted.

Brakes: Vented discs front, solid discs rear, servo-assisted.

Tyres: 235/70 HR 15.

Dimensions: Length 5370 mm (211.4 in), width 1837 mm (74.3 in), height 1485 mm (58.5 in), wheelbase 3160 mm (124.4 in).

Unladen weight: 2273 kg (5010 lb).

Performance: Maximum speed, 119 mph. 0 to 60 mph, 10.0 sec. Fuel consumption, 16.1 mpg (at constant 75 mph).

Features: Vinyl roof cover normally fitted and gives ready distinction from Silver Spirit. Outstanding comfort, quietness and refinement. Magnificent finish, and lavish standard equipment.

Identity: Diesel-powered addition to SD1 range of five-door hatchback saloons, supplementing existing six-cylinder, four-cylinder and V8 petrol engines.

Engine: Front-mounted four-cylinder with separate, individually detachable cylinders, Italian made by VM. Turbocharger standard. Bore, 92 mm, stroke 90 mm; capacity 2393 cc. Power, 90 bhp (67 kW) at 4200 rpm; torque 142 lb ft (196 Nm) at 2350 rpm. KKK turbocharger.

Transmission: Rear-wheel drive; five-speed manual transmission with very high fifth to give 30 per cent overdrive, with 3.9-to-1 axle. No automatic option for diesel. Top gear mph at 1000 rpm: 23.9.

Suspension: Front, independent, MacPherson struts, coil springs, telescopic dampers and anti-roll bar. Rear, live axle with torque tube, coil springs and Watt linkage. Boge Nivomat self-levelling strut.

Steering: Rack and pinion, power assisted.

Brakes: Discs front, drums rear, servo-assisted.

Tyres: 175 HR 14.

Dimensions: Length 4698 mm (185 in), width 1768 mm (70 in), height 1382 mm (54.4 in), wheelbase 2815 mm (110.8 in).

Unladen weight: 1495 kg (3,296 lb).

Performance: Maximum speed, 101 mph. 0 to 60 mph, 14.9 sec. Fuel consumption, 32.7 mpg (at constant 75 mph).

Features: Luxury saloon with small car fuel consumption. Generous standard equipment including electric window lifts, steel panel sunroof and central locking.

Identity: New at Birmingham 1982 initially to be built to order only. Main change is introduction of Lucas fuel injection for V8 engine. Look for spoked alloy wheels, large spoiler at rear with Vitesse name below (formerly used by Triumph).

Engine: Front-mounted V8-cylinder with all-alloy construction and hydraulic tappets. Lucas L electronic fuel injection. Compression ratio 9.75-to-1. Bore, 88.9 mm, stroke 71.1 mm; capacity 3528 cc. Power, 190 bhp (142 kW) at 5280 rpm; torque 220 lb ft (304 Nm) at 4000 rpm.

Transmission: Rear-wheel drive; five-speed manual gearbox. No automatic option for Vitesse. Final drive ratio 3.08-to-1. Top gear mph at 1000 rpm: 29.4

Suspension: Front, independent, MacPherson struts; coil springs and telescopic dampers. Anti-roll bar. Rear, torque tube live axle, with varying rate coil springs and Watts linkage; self-levelling damper units.

Steering: Rack and pinion; power assistance reduces with speed.

Brakes: Vented discs front, drums rear, servo-assisted.

Tyres: 205/60 VR 15.

Dimensions: Length 4727 mm (186.3 in), width 1768 mm (69.6 in), height 1355 mm (53.4 in), wheelbase 2815 mm (110.8 in).

Unladen weight: 1439 kg (3173 lb).

Performance (Works): Maximum speed, 135 mph. 0 to 60 mph, 7.1 sec. Fuel consumption, 30.1 mpg (at constant 75 mph).

Features: One of the fastest five-seater production cars, and still with the functional five-door body of all Rovers. Sports seats, trip computer, sunroof, radio/cassette all standard.

SAAB (S)   900 GLE

Identity: Four-door saloon (three-door version is EMS), sturdily built and refined, since 1981 available without the high-back seats which made it previously so boxed in. Extremely well engineered, with great attention to safety features.

Engine: Front-mounted four-cylinder with chain-driven ohc. Bosch fuel injection. Alloy head. Bore, 90 mm, stroke 78 mm; capacity 1985 cc. Power, 118 bhp (88 kW) at 5500 rpm; torque 123 lb ft (170 Nm) at 3700 rpm.

Transmission: Front-wheel drive; three-speed automatic transmission standard (Borg Warner). Final drive 3.79-to-1. Top gear mph at 1000 rpm: 18.7.

Suspension: Front, independent, wishbones and coil springs; telescopic dampers. Rear, dead beam axle on four links, with Panhard rod; coil springs and telescopic dampers.

Steering: Rack and pinion, power assisted.

Brakes: Discs front and rear, servo-assisted.

Tyres: 175/70 HR 15.

Dimensions: Length 4740 mm (186.6 in), width 1690 mm (66.5 in), height 1420 mm (55.9 in), wheelbase 2525 mm (99.4 in).

Unladen weight: 1257 kg (2770 lb).

Performance (Works): Maximum speed, 109 mph. Fuel consumption, 29.1 mpg (at constant 75 mph).

Features: Well-finished and fully equipped, with electric front window lifts and electric adjustment for mirrors. Heated front seats, switched on automatically on starting up at low temperatures.

SAAB (S) 900 Turbo SE

Identity: Special equipment five-door with turbocharged engine. Similar specification but with automatic transmission and four-door body available as 900 Turbo CD. Remarkable combination of speed, safety and versatility.

Engine: Front-mounted four-cylinder with chain-driven ohc. Alloy head. Garrett turbocharger and Bosch K-Jetronic fuel injection. Bore, 90 mm, stroke 78 mm; capacity 1985 cc. Power, 145 bhp (108 kW) at 5000 rpm; torque 174 lb ft (240 Nm) at 3000 rpm.

Transmission: Front-wheel drive; five-speed manual gearbox. Final drive ratio 3.08-to-1. Top gear mph at 1000 rpm: 22.6.

Suspension: Front, independent, wishbones and coil springs; telescopic dampers. Rear, dead beam axle on four trailing links, with Panhard rod; coil springs and telescopic dampers.

Steering: Rack and pinion, power assisted.

Brakes: Discs front and rear, servo-assisted.

Tyres: 195/60 HR 15.

Dimensions: Length 4739 mm (186.6 in), width 1690 mm (66.5. in), height 1420 mm (55.9 in), wheelbase 2525 mm (99.4 in).

Unladen weight: 1185 kg (2612 lb).

Performance: Maximum speed, 118 mph. 0 to 60 mph, 9.6. sec. Fuel consumption, 25.7 mpg (at constant 75 mph).

Features: Spoilers front and rear, and alloy wheels. Generously equipped car, and turbocharged engine gives excellent response for swift overtaking, yet fuel consumption very reasonable.

SBARRO (CH) Royale

Identity: One of several exclusively styled and built showpiece cars from Swiss coachbuilder Sbarro. Reminiscent of former Bugatti Royale. Other replicas of traditional models available. Twin Rover V8 engines give 7-litre capacity.

Engines: Front-mounted, 2 × V8-cylinder with hydraulic tappets and aluminium construction for blocks and heads. Bore, 88.9 mm, stroke 71.2 mm; capacity (total) 7064 cc. Power, 309 bhp (231 kW) at 5250 rpm; torque 389 lb ft (538 Nm) at 2500 rpm.

Transmission: Rear-wheel drive; three-speed automatic. Choice of transmission units, but no manual version.

Suspension: Front, independent, wishbones and torsion bars; telescopic dampers. Anti-roll bar. Rear, independent, longitudinal and transverse arms; final drive unit mounted to chassis; telescopic dampers.

Brakes: Discs front and rear, servo-assisted.

Tyres: 7 in × 18.

Dimensions: Length 6000 mm (236 in), width 1900 mm (75 in), height 2050 mm (81 in), wheelbase 3850 mm (152 in).

Unladen weight: 2750 kg (6057 lb).

Performance (Works): Maximum speed, 112 mph. 0 to 60 mph, 11.0 sec. Fuel consumption, 14 mpg (at constant 75 mph).

Features: Faithful reproduction of the Bugatti Royale bodywork with modern running gear and chassis. Striking appearance and immaculate finish.

SKODA (CS)   120LSE

Identity: Low price is the special attraction of this rear-engined car, but in respect of handling and stability it has all the disadvantages of high mass and swing axles at the rear end, and needs to be driven with care on corners. Three versions offered, plus 105S with 1046 engine.

Engine: Rear-mounted four-cylinder with pushrod ohv. Jikov carb. Alloy block. Engine in-line at rear, inclined to right. Bore, 72 mm, stroke 72 mm; capacity 1174 cc. Power, 58 bhp (43 kW) at 5200 rpm; torque 67 lb ft (90 Nm) at 3250 rpm.

Transmission: Rear-wheel drive; four-speed manual gearbox. No automatic option. Top gear mph at 1000 rpm: 16.7.

Suspension: Front, independent, wishbones and coil springs; telescopic dampers. Anti-roll bar. Rear, independent, swing axles and leading arms; coil springs and telescopic dampers.

Steering: Worm and nut.

Brakes: Discs front, drums rear, servo-assisted.

Tyres: 165 SR 13.

Dimensions: Length 4160 mm (163.8 in), width 1595 mm (62.8 in), height 1400 mm (55.1 in), wheelbase 2400 mm (94.5 in).

Unladen weight: 885 kg (1951 lb).

Performance: Maximum speed, 84 mph. 0 to 60 mph, 18.9 sec. Fuel consumption, 32.5 mpg (at constant 75 mph).

Features: Tilt or lift-out sunroof; rev counter; vinyl roof covering; radio/cassette. Four headlamps.

SUBARU (J)   1800 4WD

Identity: Unusual car with special appeal for vets, farmers and others who have to be able to tackle dirt roads in winter and not get stuck. Front wheel drive standard, and 4WD version (saloon or estate) has advantage that rear drive can be selected in addition.

Engine: Front-mounted four-cylinder with horizontally opposed layout; central camshaft. Alloy construction for heads and block. Bore, 92 mm, stroke 67 mm; capacity 1782 cc. Power, 79 bhp (59kW) at 5200 rpm; torque 98 lb ft (135 Nm) at 2400 rpm.

Transmission: Four-wheel drive; main drive to front wheels, selectable drive to rear wheels. Four-speed manual gearbox. Top gear mph at 1000 rpm: 19.1.

Suspension: Front, independent, MacPherson struts, coil springs and telescopic dampers. Anti-roll bar. Rear, independent, semi-trailing arms and torsion bars; telescopic dampers.

Steering: Rack and pinion.

Brakes: Discs front, drums rear, servo-assisted.

Tyres: 155 R 13.

Dimensions: Length 4275 mm (168.3 in), width 1620 mm (63.8 in), height 1445 mm (56.9 in), wheelbase 2446 mm (96.3 in).

Unladen weight: 1020 kg (2249 lb).

Performance: Maximum speed, 90 mph. 0 to 60 mph, 16.3 sec. Fuel consumption, 28.1 mpg (overall).

Features: Surprisingly rugged car, intended for hard work. Frameless glass side windows. 1982 models identified by four oblong headlamps. Rather pronounced forward overhang, and severe understeer, but acceptable handling for a car of this versatility.

SUZUKI (J)   **Alto**

Identity: Fascinating and neatly engineered Japanese baby car. Two-door with lift-up rear hatch. Very economical. Some markets also get four-door 543 cc saloon (Fronte), and the 970 cc coupé (Cervo).

Engine: Front-mounted three-cylinder with belt-driven ohc. Mikuni-Solex carb. Alloy head. Bore, 68.5 mm, stroke 72 mm; capacity 796 cc. Power, 39 bhp (29 kW) at 5500 rpm; torque 43 lb ft (60 Nm) at 3000 rpm.

Transmission: Front-wheel drive; four-speed manual gearbox. Final drive ratio 4.35-to-1. Top gear mph at 1000 rpm: 14.7.

Suspension: Front, independent, MacPherson struts and coil springs; telescopic dampers. Anti-roll bar. Rear, dead beam axle on semi-elliptic leaf springs. Telescopic dampers. Coupé has independent rear suspension.

Steering: Rack and pinion.

Brakes: Drums front and rear; front discs optional.

Tyres: 145/70 SR 12.

Dimensions: Length 3294 mm (129.7 in), width 1405 mm (55.3 in), height 1336 mm (52.6 in), wheelbase 2151 mm (84.7 in).

Unladen weight: 630 kg (1389 lb).

Performance: Maximum speed, 82 mph. 0 to 60 mph, 15.8 sec. Fuel consumption, 47.9 mpg (at constant 56 mph).

Features: Very basic little economy car and lacking the sure-footed refinement and handling qualities of the Mini, but quite lively and simple to drive.

SUZUKI (J)   SJ410Q

Suzuki SJ410Q Soft Top version

Identity: This complex title identifies the impressive little Suzuki cross-country car. Ideal for farmers and others who need a small, compact personnel carrier with seats for no more than two, yet with four-wheel drive off-road ability.

Engine: Front-mounted four-cylinder with single belt-driven ohc. Alloy head. Front, in-line, installation. Bore, 65.5 mm, stroke 72 mm; capacity 970 cc. Power, 47 bhp (35 kW) at 5000 rpm; torque 61 lb ft (84 Nm) at 3000 rpm.

Transmission: Four-wheel drive; four-speed manual gearbox. Normal drive to rear wheels; four-wheel drive selector adds front drive. Low ratio transfer gearbox for severe conditions. Top gear mph at 1000 rpm: 17.9.

Suspension: Front, live axle on semi-elliptic leaf springs. Telescopic dampers. Rear, live axle on semi-elliptic leaf springs. Telescopic dampers.

Steering: Rack and pinion.

Brakes: Drums front and rear, front discs optional.

Tyres: 195 SR 15.

Dimensions: Length 3430 mm (135 in), width 1460 mm (57.5 in), height 1690 mm (66.5 in), wheelbase 2030 mm (80 in).

Unladen weight: 830 kg (1830 lb).

Performance: Maximum speed, 68 mph. Fuel consumption, 25.3 mpg (overall).

Features: Impressive cross-country ability. Easy to drive. Choice of tilt cover or hardtop. Effective utility vehicle without the heavy running costs incurred by larger 4 × 4 vehicles.

TALBOT (GB, F) Horizon LD

Identity: Additional version of four-door front-drive hatchback model with transverse-mounted diesel engine; all-new unit of 1905 cc capacity, introduced Paris 1982, and on British market from Birmingham Show. Special attention to noise levels.

Engine: Front-mounted four-cylinder with glass-fibre reinforced dog tooth drive to camshaft in head, also driving injection pump. Compression ratio 23.5-to-1. Bore, 83 mm, stroke 88 mm; capacity 1905 cc. Power, 64 bhp (48 kW) at 4600 rpm; torque 88 lb ft (122 Nm) at 2000 rpm.

Transmission: Front-wheel drive; choice of four-speed or five-speed manual gearbox (no automatic transmission available). Top gear mph at 1000 rpm: 21.0 (4-speed); 21.5 (5-speed).

Suspension: Front, independent, wishbones and longitudinal torsion bars; telescopic dampers. Anti-roll bar. Rear, independent, trailing arms and coil springs; telescopic dampers. Anti-roll bar.

Steering: Rack and pinion.

Brakes: Discs front, drums rear, servo-assisted (pressure hydraulics).

Tyres: 145 SR 13.

Dimensions: Length 3960 mm (155.9 in), width 1679 mm (66.1 in), height 1410 mm (55.5 in), wheelbase 2520 mm (99.2 in).

Unladen weight: 1020 kg (2249 lb).

Performance (Works, 5-speed gearbox): Maximum speed, 97 mph. 0 to 60 mph, 17.9 sec. Fuel consumption, 44.1 mpg (at constant 75 mph).

Features: Significant new contender bringing advanced diesel technology to small cars. Copper radiator has two fans, and there is an overheating alarm behind facia. Well furnished and equipped.

TALBOT (F)

Matra Murena

Identity: Unusual sports car with three-abreast seating; successor to the Bagheera model, with aerodynamic two-door hatchback body. Mid-engined layout. Available only with left-hand drive, and not imported to Britain. Choice of 1.6-litre (detailed below) or 2.2.-litre engine.

Engine: Mid-mounted four-cylinder with alloy head. Pushrod ohv. Weber twin-choke carb. Transverse installation. Bore, 80.6 mm, stroke 78 mm; capacity 1592 cc. Power, 90 bhp (67.5 kW) at 5600 rpm; torque 96 lb ft (132 Nm) at 3200 rpm.

Transmission: Rear-wheel drive; five.speed manual gearbox. Final drive ratio 4.77-to-1. Top gear mph at 1000 rpm: 19.7.

Suspension: Front, independent, wishbones and torsion bars; telescopic dampers. Anti-roll bar. Rear, independent, semi-trailing arms and coil springs; telescopic dampers. Anti-roll bar.

Steering: Rack and pinion.

Brakes: Discs front and rear, servo-assisted.

Tyres: 185/60 HR 14 (front), 195/60 HR 14 (rear).

Dimensions: Length 4070 mm (160.2 in), width 1750 mm (68.9 in), height 1220 mm (48 in), wheelbase 2435 mm (95.9 in).

Unladen weight: 1000 kg (2204 lb).

Performance (Works): Maximum speed, 113 mph. 0 to 60 mph, 11.8 sec. Fuel consumption, 38.7 mpg (at constant 75 mph).

Features: Glass fibre body on steel chassis. Electronic ignition introduced Paris 1982, and latest version is identified by internal door pockets. Velour upholstery. 2.2 has central locking.

TALBOT (F, GB)   Samba Cabriolet

Identity: Familiar chunky shape of Talbot's charming little economy car, in convertible guise with fixed roll bar. Launched October 1981, and on the British market, Birmingham 1982.

Engine: Front-mounted four-cylinder with transverse mounting, and inclined rearward at 72 deg angle. Alloy head and block. Ohc. Bore, 75 mm, stroke 77 mm; capacity 1361 cc. Power, 71 bhp (53 kW) at 6000 rpm; torque 77 lb ft (107 Nm) at 3000 rpm.

Transmission: Front-wheel drive; four-speed gearbox, all indirect. Final drive 3.56-to-1. Top gear mph at 1000 rpm: 20.0.

Suspension: Front, independent, MacPherson struts and coil springs; telescopic dampers; anti-roll bar. Rear, independent, trailing arms, coil springs and telescopic dampers.

Steering: Rack and pinion.

Brakes: Discs front, drums rear, servo-assisted.

Tyres: 165/70 SR 13.

Dimensions: Length 3505 mm (138 in), width 1530 mm (60 in), height 1360 mm (53.5 in), wheelbase 2340 mm (92 in).

Unladen weight: 850 kg (1872 lb).

Performance (Works): Maximum speed, 99 mph. 0 to 60 mph, 12.5 sec. Fuel consumption, 40.4 mpg (at constant 75 mph).

Features: Welcome addition to all-too-limited choice of open cars; easy to drive, good handling, hood quite simple to put up or down, and outstanding economy.

TALBOT (F, GB)   Tagora 2.2 GLS

Identity: Spacious five-seater three-box saloon of conventional layout, with choice of 2.2- or 2.7-litre petrol engines, or 2.3-litre turbo diesel. 4-cyl 2.2 (detailed below) offers particularly good economy in relation to size of car.

Engine: Front-mounted four-cylinder with alloy head, chain-driven single ohc. Electronic ignition. Compression 9.5-to-1. Bore, 91.7 mm, stroke 81.6 mm; capacity 2155 cc. Power, 113 bhp (85 kW) at 5400 rpm torque 133 lb ft (184 Nm) at 3200 rpm.

Transmission: Rear-wheel drive; five-speed gearbox standard. Basic version (GL) gets four-speed. Three-speed automatic available. Top gear mph at 1000 rpm: 22.5.

Suspension: Front, independent, MacPherson struts; coil springs and telescopic dampers. Anti-roll bar. Rear, independent, trailing arms and coil springs; telescopic dampers. Anti-roll bar.

Steering: Rack and pinion, power assisted on GLS.

Brakes: Discs front, drums rear, servo-assisted.

Tyres: 175 SR 14.

Dimensions: Length 4628 mm (128.2 in), width 1811 mm (71.3 in), height 1445 mm (56.9 in), wheelbase 2809 mm (110.6 in).

Unladen weight: 1255 kg (2767 lb).

Performance: Maximum speed, 106 mph. 0 to 60 mph, 11.3 sec. Fuel consumption, 29.4 mpg (at constant 75 mph).

Features: Very comfortable and relaxing car, giving easy, quiet cruising and extremely good ride. Well-equipped in GLS form.

TOYOTA (J)   Celica 2.0 Liftback

Identity: Stylish coupé with lamps set back from horizontal, tilt forward for use when switched on. Car available as hatchback (called the Liftback) or as the St Coupé, with separate boot.

Engine: Front-mounted four-cylinder with chain-driven ohc, electronic ignition, and Aisan twin-choke carb. Iron block, alloy head. Bore, 84 mm, stroke 89 mm; capacity 1972 cc. Power, 103 bhp (77 kW) at 5000 rpm; torque 116 lb ft (160 Nm) at 4000 rpm.

Transmission: Rear-wheel drive; five-speed gearbox standard, with Hypoid 3.91-to-1 final drive. Four-speed automatic available. Top gear mph at 1000 rpm: 20.9.

Suspension: Front, independent, MacPherson struts; coil springs and telescopic dampers; anti-roll bar. Rear, independent, semi-trailing arms and coil springs; telescopic dampers; anti-roll bar.

Steering: Rack and pinion.

Brakes: Discs front, drums rear, servo-assisted.

Tyres: 185/70 SR 14.

Dimensions: Length 4435 mm (170.6 in), width 1665 mm (65.6 in), height 1320 mm (52 in), wheelbase 2500 mm (98.4 in).

Unladen weight: 1170 kg (2576 lb).

Performance: Maximum speed, 109 mph. 0 to 60 mph, 10.5 sec. Fuel consumption, 31.5 mpg (at constant 75 mph).

Features: Very pleasing touring car, with emphasis more on the comfort side than on sporting behaviour, but very well equipped and furnished and a pleasure to drive.

TOYOTA (J)   Corolla 1.6SR Coupé

Identity: Corolla sells in huge volumes worldwide, and included here is the sporting version with most powerful of the 1600 cc engines. Also available as Liftback, with less power. Corolla range includes two-or four-door saloon or four-door estate, all with 1290 engine.

Engine: Front-mounted four-cylinder with chain-driven ohc; twin Aisan carbs. Compression 9.4-to-1. Alloy head. Bore, 85 mm, stroke 70 mm; capacity 1588 cc. Power, 86 bhp (64 kW) at 5600 rpm; torque 87 lb ft (120 Nm) at 4000 rpm.

Transmission: Rear-wheel drive; manual five-speed gearbox—no automatic option for 1600 Corolla in Britain. Top gear mph at 1000 rpm: 20.0.

Suspension: Front, independent, MacPherson struts; coil springs and telescopic dampers. Anti-roll bar. Rear, live axle on four trailing links with Panhard rod; coil springs and telescopic dampers.

Steering: Recirculating ball.

Brakes: Discs front, drums rear, servo-assisted.

Tyres: 165 SR 13.

Dimensions: Length 4105 mm (161.6 in), width 1625 mm (64 in), height 1335 mm (52.6 in), wheelbase 2400 mm (94.5 in).

Unladen weight: 950 kg (2095 lb).

Performance: Maximum speed, 98 mph. 0 to 60 mph, 12.5 sec. Fuel consumption, 30.1 mpg (at constant 75 mph).

Features: Two-door body with opening rear hatch. Striped fabric upholstery, and individually folding rear seats. Tailgate wash/wipe and digital quartz clock.

TOYOTA (J)   Land-Cruiser

Identity: Cross-country vehicle in the Toyota range with big estate car body. Not as competent as a Range Rover, but with the advantages of being much cheaper and having diesel availability.

Engine: Front-mounted six-cylinder with alloy head; pushrod ohv. Compression 19.0-to-1. Diesel injection by Toyota. Bore, 91 mm, stroke 102 mm; capacity 3980 cc. Power, 103 bhp (77 kW) at 3500 rpm; torque 177 lb ft (245 Nm) at 2300 rpm.

Transmission: Four-wheel drive; four-speed manual gearbox. Normal drive to rear wheels, plus selectable front drive. Low ratio transfer gearbox, to all four wheels. No automatic option. Top gear mph at 1000 rpm: 22.6.

Suspension: Front, live axle on semi-elliptic leaf springs. Telescopic dampers. Rear, live axle on semi-elliptic leaf springs. Telescopic dampers.

Steering: Recirculating ball, power assisted.

Brakes: Discs front, drums rear, servo-assisted (pressure hydraulics).

Tyres: 205 SR 13.

Dimensions: Length 4675 mm (184.1 in), width 1800 mm (70.9 in), height 1800 mm (70.9 in), wheelbase 2730 mm (107.5 in).

Unladen weight: 1940 kg (4267 lb).

Performance: Maximum speed, 85 mph. 0 to 60 mph, 19.3 sec. Fuel consumption, 23.0 mpg (overall).

Features: Good cross-country performance and refined interior without seeming too much a utility vehicle. Easy to drive in spite of its bulk. Some limitations of steering and cornering. Two-piece tailgate; four side doors.

TOYOTA (J)   Supra 2.8i

Identity: Exciting new version of the Celica Coupé, launched in Britain August 1982. Similar body, but with different front, and pop-up headlamps in place of Celica's 'tilt' lamps. Powerful injection engine gives terrific performance to rival top GT cars.

Engine: Front-mounted six-cylinder with twin ohc driven by toothed belt. Breakerless ignition and Nippondenso injection. Bore, 83 mm, stroke 85 mm; capacity 2759 cc. Power, 168 bhp (125 kW) at 5600 rpm; torque 169 lb ft (286 Nm) at 4600 rpm.

Transmission: Rear-wheel drive; five-speed manual gearbox—no automatic option for Supra, although it is available for Celica. Top gear mph at 1000 rpm: 22.6.

Suspension: Front, independent, MacPherson struts, coil springs and telescopic dampers. Anti-roll bar. Rear, independent, semi-trailing arms; coil springs and telescopic dampers. Anti-roll bar.

Steering: Rack and pinion, power assisted.

Brakes: Vented discs front and rear, servo-assisted.

Tyres: 195/70 VR 14.

Dimensions: Length 4620 mm (182 in), width 1685 mm (66.3 in), height 1315 mm (51.8 in), wheelbase 2615 mm (103 in).

Unladen weight: 1302 kg (2870 lb).

Performance: Maximum speed, 131 mph. 0 to 60 mph, 8.7 sec. Fuel consumption, 27.4 mpg (at constant 75 mph).

Features: Impressive facia layout with 'half moon' instruments. Two-door hatchback body, with divided, folding, rear seats. Well-equipped and rewarding to drive.

TOYOTA (J)   Tercel GL

Identity: First front-drive Toyota to be offered in Britain; launched Birmingham 1982. Compact and neatly-styled hatchback with choice of three or five doors. Engine mounted in line and inclined to the left. Oblong headlamps and corner indicators. Sidelamps recessed in polypropylene front bumper/air dam moulding.

Engine: Front-mounted four-cylinder with single ohc. Aisin twin-choke carb. Compression ratio 9.3-to-1 (two-star regular fuel). Bore, 76 mm, stroke 71.4 mm; capacity 1295 cc. Power, 64.3 bhp (48 kW) at 6000 rpm; torque 73 lb ft (101 Nm) at 3800 rpm.

Transmission: Front-wheel drive; five-speed manual gearbox standard. Three-speed automatic optional. Final drive ratio 3.73-to-1. Top gear mph at 1000 rpm: 21.4.

Suspension: Front, independent, MacPherson struts with offset spring-damper centre-lines; coil springs and telescopic dampers. Anti-roll bar. Rear, independent, MacPherson struts with parallel transverse lower arms; coil springs and gas-filled telescopic dampers.

Steering: Rack and pinion.

Brakes: Discs front, drums rear, servo-assisted.

Tyres: 155 SR 13.

Dimensions: Length 3881 mm (152.8 in), width 1615 mm (63.6 in), height 1389 mm (54.7 in), wheelbase 2430 mm (95.7 in).

Unladen weight: 895 kg (1975 lb).

Performance (Works): Maximum speed, 92 mph. 0 to 60 mph, 13.4 sec. Fuel consumption, 34.3 mpg (at constant 75 mph).

Features: Quartz clock, radio, tinted glass and rear wash/wipe all standard. Mid-split rear seat.

TRIUMPH (GB)   Acclaim CD

Identity: Controversial British-assembled version of Japanese Honda Ballade. Three-box saloon with imported engine and fwd transmission package. Attractive package overall, with all-alloy engine, five-speed gearbox, all-independent suspension; outstanding economy.

Engine: Front-mounted four-cylinder with belt-driven ohc; alloy block and head; breakerless ignition; twin Keihin cv carbs. Bore, 72 mm, stroke 82 mm; capacity 1335 cc. Power, 70 bhp (52 kW) at 5750 rpm; torque 74 lb ft (102 Nm) at 3500 rpm.

Transmission: Front-wheel drive; five-speed gearbox standard; three-speed semi-automatic optional. Spur gear final drive. Top gear mph at 1000 rpm: 19.8.

Suspension: Front, independent, MacPherson struts; coil springs and telescopic dampers. Anti-roll bar. Rear, independent, MacPherson struts; coil springs and telescopic dampers.

Steering: Rack and pinion.

Brakes: Discs front, drums rear, servo-assisted.

Tyres: 155 SR 13.

Dimensions: Length 4095 mm (161.2 in), width 1600 mm (63 in), height 1340 mm (52.7 in), wheelbase 2320 mm (91.3 in).

Unladen weight: 821 kg (1810 lb).

Performance: Maximum speed, 92 mph (fourth). 0 to 60 mph, 12.9 sec. Fuel consumption, 34.0 mpg (at constant 75 mph).

Features: Four versions available, all mechanically the same but different equipment. CD has headlamp washers. HLS is best value of all. Three-box saloon; on top models, rear seat panel gives boot access.

TVR (GB)   **Tasmin convertible**

Identity: Two-seater sports car with impressively clean body styling, introduced Brussels 1980. Other bodies are coupé (as first launched), and longer 2+2 coupé. Ford Cologne 2.8-litre engine (detailed below) or (since October 1981) four-cylinder 2-litre.

Engine: Front-mounted V6-cylinder with cast iron heads and block; pushrod ohv. Bosch K-Jetronic fuel injection. Bore, 93 mm, stroke 68.5 mm; capacity 2792 cc. Power, 160 bhp (120 kW) at 5700 rpm; torque 162 lb ft (224 Nm) at 4300 rpm.

Transmission: Rear-wheel drive; four-speed manual gearbox. Three-speed automatic optional. Final drive ratio 3.07-to-1. Top gear mph at 1000 rpm: 22.1.

Suspension: Front, independent, MacPherson struts; coil springs and telescopic dampers. Anti-roll bar. Rear, independent, trailing arms, and fixed length drive shafts. Coil springs and telescopic dampers.

Steering: Rack and pinion.

Brakes: Discs front and rear, servo-assisted.

Tyres: 205/60 VR 14.

Dimensions: Length 4013 mm (158 in), width 1728 mm (68 in), height 1192 mm (47 in), wheelbase 2387 mm (94 in).

Unladen weight: 1017 kg (2242 lb).

Performance: Maximum speed, 124 mph. 0 to 60 mph, 7.8 sec. Fuel consumption, 20.7 mpg (overall).

Features: One of the best convertibles of all for ease of changing to fully up or fully open: over-centre supports secure rear hood, and roof panel is removable. Instruments rather small, but finish good.

VAUXHALL (GB, D)   Astra SR 1600S

Identity: Also in the Opel range on the Continent as the Kadett, the Astra is a chunky, efficiently-packaged small front-drive car with transverse engine and fwd (GM's first fwd car), available in hatchback or estate car form, with three or five doors.

Engine: Front-mounted four-cylinder with belt-driven ohc. Alloy head. Electronic ignition. Transverse installation. Bore, 80 mm, stroke 79.5 mm; capacity 1598 cc. Power, 88 bhp (66 kW) at 5800 rpm; torque 91 lb ft (126 Nm) at 3800 rpm.

Transmission: Front-wheel drive; five-speed manual gearbox standard on SR—optional on all other Astras which have four-speed gearbox standard. Three-speed automatic also available (but not SR). Top gear mph at 1000 rpm: 24.8.

Suspension: Front, independent, MacPherson struts; coil springs and telescopic dampers. Anti-roll bar. Rear, dead beam axle on trailing arms; coil springs and telescopic dampers. Anti-roll bar.

Steering: Rack and pinion.

Brakes: Discs front, drums rear, servo-assisted.

Tyres: 155 SR 13.

Dimensions: Length 4000 mm (157.5 in), width 1638 mm (64.5 in), height 1384 mm (54.5 in), wheelbase 2515 mm (99 in).

Unladen weight: 855 kg (1884 lb).

Performance: Maximum speed, 105 mph (fourth). 0 to 60 mph, 10.8 sec. Fuel consumption, 38.1 mpg (at constant 75 mph).

Features: Improved specifications from September 1982, including laminated screen, tailgate wash/wipe, three-speed heater fan, and two-way door and ignition key system for all models. Black grille and deep front spoiler identify SR.

Vauxhall (GB) Cavalier LD

Identity: Very successful front-drive four-door saloon or five-door hatchback, launched 1981 at Frankfurt, and available since 1982 with 1600 diesel engine. Also produced in Germany as the Opel Ascona.

Engine: Front-mounted four-cylinder with single ohc and self-venting Bosch diesel injection, on 23-to-1 compression. Bore, 80 mm, stroke 79.5 mm; capacity 1598 cc. Power, 54 bhp (40 kW) at 4600 rpm; torque 71 lb ft (98 Nm) at 2400 rpm.

Transmission: Front-wheel drive; four-speed gearbox and s.d.p. clutch; final drive, 3.74-to-1. Five-speed optional since September 1982. Top gear mph at 1000 rpm: 18.5.

Suspension: Front, independent, MacPherson struts, telescopic dampers; anti-roll bar. Rear, dead beam axle on trailing arms and torsion beam; coil springs and telescopic dampers; anti-roll bar.

Steering: Rack and pinion.

Brakes: Discs front, drums rear, servo-assisted.

Tyres: 165 SR 13.

Dimensions: Length 4366 mm (172 in), width 1668 mm (65.7 in), height 1395 mm (55 in), wheelbase 2574 mm (101 in).

Unladen weight: 1045 kg (2299 lb).

Performance: Maximum speed, 87 mph. 0 to 60 mph, 17.8 sec. Fuel consumption, 38.1 mpg (at constant 75 mph).

Features: Very straightforward and easy car to drive, with excellent accommodation and road manners, and diesel engine which is unobtrusive most of the time, except at tickover and in manoeuvring. Little 'diesel penalty'—big economy gains.

VAUXHALL (GB, D) Carlton

Identity: New version of Vauxhall Carlton with similar body, different front, stylish new wheels and wider engine choice introduced Birmingham 1982. Four-door saloon or five-door estate. New 1800 engine (details follow), or former 2-litre cam-in-head unit; 2.3-litre diesel also available.

Engine: Front-mounted four-cylinder with alloy head and belt-driven ohc. Hydraulic tappets. GMF Varajet carburettor. Compression ratio 9.2-to-1. Bore, 84.8 mm, stroke 79.5 mm; capacity 1795 cc. Power, 90 bhp (67 kW) at 5400 rpm; torque 106 lb ft (146 Nm) at 3000 rpm.

Transmission: Rear-wheel drive; five-speed manual gearbox standard; three-speed automatic optional, with anti-slip lock-up clutch. Top gear mph at 1000 rpm: 24.1.

Suspension: Front, independent, MacPherson struts; coil springs and telescopic dampers. Anti-roll bar. Rear, live axle on trailing links with lateral track bar; coil springs and telescopic dampers. Anti-roll bar.

Steering: Recirculating ball, power assisted.

Brakes: Discs front, drums rear, servo-assisted.

Tyres: 175 SR 14.

Dimensions: Length 4653 mm (183.2 in), width 1725 mm (67.9 in), height 1387 mm (54.6 in), wheelbase 2667 mm (105 in).

Unladen weight: 1115 kg (2458 lb)

Performance: No data available, on closing for press. Fuel consumption, 35.8 mpg (at constant 75 mph).

Features: Generously equipped with central locking (GL), radio/cassette, internally-adjustable door mirrors, and electric boot release.

VOLKSWAGEN (D)   Golf GLi

Identity: Convertible version of Golf. Hood folds down quite easily and locks into place in well; detachable tonneau cover provided. Engine increased to 1800, Paris 1982. Five-speed gearbox standard.

Engine: Front-mounted four-cylinder with Bosch K-Jetronic fuel injection. Alloy head. Transverse installation. Bore, 81 mm, stroke 86.4 mm; capacity 1781 cc. Power, 112 bhp (82 kW) at 5900 rpm; torque 107 lb ft (148 Nm) at 3500 rpm.

Transmission: Front-wheel drive; five-speed gearbox. Three-speed automatic available for GL version, but not for GLi. Top gear mph at 1000 rpm: 23.6.

Suspension: Front, independent, MacPherson struts and coil springs; telescopic dampers. Anti-roll bar. Rear, independent, trailing arms and coil springs; telescopic dampers.

Steering: Rack and pinion.

Brakes: Discs front, drums rear, servo-assisted.

Tyres: 175/70 HR 13.

Dimensions: Length 3815 mm (150.2 in), width 1628 mm (64.1 in), height 1394 mm (54.9 in), wheelbase 2400 mm (94.5 in).

Unladen weight: 940 kg (2072 lb).

Performance (est.): Maximum speed, 110 mph. 0 to 60 mph, 10.0 sec. Fuel consumption, 28 mpg (overall).

Features: Clever provision for glass rear window, with heating element, in folding hood. Padded roll-over bar. Alloy wheels. Halogen headlamps. Superbly smooth engine.

VOLKSWAGEN (D)   Passat CL Formel E

Identity: Body comes as hatchback or estate car—all with five doors. Choice of 1600 four-cylinder engine or five-cylinder 2-litre. Formel E specification is available only for the 1600, but five-speed (4+E) gearbox available for ordinary 1600 versions as an extra. Diesel engine alternative, also 1600.

Engine: Front-mounted four-cylinder with ohc driven by toothed belt. In-line installation. Alloy head. Compression 8.2-to-1. Bore, 79.5 mm, stroke 80.0 mm; capacity 1588 cc. Power, 75 bhp (56 kW) at 5600 rpm; torque 89 lb ft (123 Nm) at 3200 rpm.

Transmission: Front-wheel drive; five-speed gearbox, with 'change-up' warning light, and fifth intended to be used as much as possible for optimum economy. Top gear mph at 1000 rpm: 22.5.

Suspension: Front, independent, MacPherson struts; coil springs and telescopic dampers. Anti-roll bar. Rear, semi-independent, trailing arms and torsion beam; coil springs and telescopic dampers. Torsion beam gives anti-roll effect.

Steering: Rack and pinion.

Brakes: Discs front, drums rear, servo-assisted.

Tyres: 165 SR 13.

Dimensions: Length 4435 mm (174.6 in), width 1685 mm (66.3 in), height 1385 mm (54.5 in), wheelbase 2550 mm (100.4 in).

Unladen weight: 991 kg (2185 lb).

Performance: Maximum speed, 102 mph (fourth). 0 to 60 mph, 11.9 sec. Fuel consumption, 35.8 mpg (at constant 75 mph).

Features: Comfortable and practical car with very good economy. Neat finish. Good load capacity (payload 490 kg).

VOLKSWAGEN (D) Polo C Formel E

Identity: Revised and re-bodied version of Volkswagen's smallest model, introduced Frankfurt 1981. Semi-estate car body style; also available as three-box saloon in Polo Classic. Choice of 1043 or two versions of 1093 engine. Formel E has the more powerful 1093 and higher gearing.

Engine: Front-mounted four-cylinder in-line engine, transversely mounted. Single belt-driven overhead camshaft. Bore, 69.5 mm, stroke 72 mm; capacity 1093 cc. Power, 50 bhp (37 kW) at 5600 rpm; torque 60 lb ft (83 Nm) at 3300 rpm.

Transmission: Front-wheel drive; four-speed gearbox with high-geared fourth labelled E for Economy. Top gear mph at 1000 rpm: 19.6.

Suspension: Front, independent, MacPherson struts, telescopic dampers, anti-roll bar. Rear, semi-independent, trailing arms and torsion beam, telescopic dampers; torsion beam provides anti-roll effect.

Steering: Rack and pinion.

Brakes: Discs front, drums rear, no servo.

Tyres: 145 SR 13.

Dimensions: Length 3655 mm (144 in), width 1580 mm (62 in), height 1355 mm (53 in), wheelbase 2335 mm (92 in).

Unladen weight: 700 kg (1540 lb).

Performance: Maximum speed, 87 mph. 0 to 60 mph, 16.7 sec. Fuel consumption, 42.2 mpg (at constant 75 mph).

Features: Crisp, tidy handling and eager performance with outstanding fuel economy, but a lot of gear changing needed, due to high ratios.

VOLKSWAGEN (D)   Santana GX5

Identity: Distinguished four-door five-seater saloon, largest in Volkswagen range, excluding Audis. Several engines and trim packs in Germany, but only GX5 on market in Britain. Wrapround bumpers and side rubbing strip, plus flarings round wheel arches.

Engine: Front-mounted five-cylinder with belt-driven single ohc. Alloy head. Solex carb. Breakerless ignition. Compression 10.0-to-1. Bore, 79.5 mm, stroke 77.4 mm; capacity 1921 cc. Power, 115 bhp (86 kW) at 5900 rpm; torque 113 lb ft. (156 Nm) at 3700 rpm.

Transmission: Front-wheel drive; five-speed (marked 4 + E) gearbox. Three-speed automatic optional. Hypoid bevel final drive, 4.9-to-1. Top gear mph at 1000 rpm: 25.4.

Suspension: Front, independent, MacPherson struts; coil springs and telescopic dampers. Rear, dead beam torsion crank axle on trailing arms; coil springs and telescopic dampers.

Steering: Rack and pinion, power assisted.

Brakes: Discs front, drums rear, servo-assisted.

Tyres: 195/60 HR 14.

Dimensions: Length 4545 mm (178.9 in), width 1695 mm (66.7 in), height 1400 mm (55.1 in), wheelbase 2550 mm (100.4 in).

Unladen weight: 1111 kg (2443 lb).

Performance: Maximum speed, 111 mph (fourth). 0 to 60 mph, 10.8 sec. Fuel consumption, 33.2 mpg (at constant 75 mph).

Features: Comfortable and extremely well-equipped car. Halogen headlamps with pressure jet washers; fog lamps (also halogen). Electric front window lifts. Fuel 'econ' gauge and gear change-up indicator light.

VOLKSWAGEN (D)

Scirocco GTi

Identity: Later version of the car which marked Volkswagen's first adventure into fwd. Attractively styled new body appeared Geneva 1981; updated to 1800 cc Paris 1982. Spoiler on rear, across lower part of window, with 'Scirocco' lettering for top models.

Engine: Front-mounted four-cylinder with Bosch K-Jetronic fuel injection. Alloy head on cast iron block. Engine mounted transversely. Bore, 81 mm, stroke 86.4 mm; capacity 1781 cc. Power, 112 bhp (82 kW) at 5900 rpm; torque 107 lb ft (148 Nm) at 3500 rpm.

Transmission: Front-wheel drive; five-speed gearbox standard; no automatic option for this version, but there is for GL. Top gear mph at 1000 rpm: 23.6.

Suspension: Front, independent, MacPherson struts and coil springs; telescopic dampers. Rear, dead beam axle on trailing arms; coil springs and telescopic dampers.

Steering: Rack and pinion.

Brakes: Discs front, drums rear, servo-assisted.

Tyres: 175/70 SR 13.

Dimensions: Length 4050 mm (159.4 in), width 1625 mm (63.9 in), height 1306 mm (51.4 in), wheelbase 2400 mm (94.4 in).

Unladen weight: 912 kg (2009 lb).

Performance (Works): Maximum speed, 118 mph (fourth). 0 to 60 mph, 9.5 sec. Fuel consumption, 35.8 mpg (at constant 75 mph).

Features: Very taut feeling car, with excellent handling, positive steering, and delightfully smooth and free-revving engine. Interior typical VW—very neat, but slightly plain. Alloy wheels.

VOLVO (S)   360GLT

Identity: Additional model in Volvo range created by fitting elderly but up-dated B19 engine in 300-Series body, with choice of three or five doors. In-line engine with drive to rear transaxle as for 343 and 345, which continue. Look for GLS (carburettor version) or GLT (injection, detailed below) lettering on grille.

Engine: Front-mounted four-cylinder with chain-driven single ohc. Bosch LE-Jetronic fuel injection. Compression 10-to-1. Bore, 89.9 mm, stroke 80 mm; capacity 1986 cc. Power, 115 bhp (86 kW) at 6000 rpm; torque 116 lb ft (160 Nm) at 3600 rpm.

Transmission: Rear-wheel drive; five-speed manual gearbox in transaxle at rear. No automatic option. Final drive ratio 3.64-to-1. Top gear mph at 1000 rpm: 21.6.

Suspension: Front, independent, MacPherson struts; coil springs and telescopic dampers. Anti-roll bar. Rear, De Dion layout with trailing arms, semi-elliptic leaf springs and telescopic dampers.

Steering: Rack and pinion.

Brakes: Discs front, drums rear, servo-assisted.

Tyres: 185/60 HR 14.

Dimensions: Length 4300 mm (169.3 in), width 1660 mm (65.4 in), height 1392 mm (54.8 in), wheelbase 2395 mm (94.3 in).

Unladen weight: 1131 kg (2493 lb).

Performance (Works): Maximum speed, 112 mph. 0 to 60 mph, 10.7 sec. Fuel consumption, 32.1 mg (at constant 75 mph).

Features: Auxiliary driving lamps standard on 360GLT, but not on GLS, so this is identity feature. Generous standard equipment.

VOLVO (S)   760 GLE

Identity: Top model of Volvo range with distinctive, squared-up but roomy body, with V6 petrol engine (details follow) or turbocharged straight-six 2.4-litre diesel.

Engine: Front-mounted V6-cylinder with block and heads in aluminium, and Bosch fuel injection. Bore, 91 mm, stroke 73 mm; capacity 2849 cc. Power, 156 bhp (116 kW) at 5700 rpm; torque 170 lb ft (235 Nm) at 3000 rpm.

Transmission: Rear-wheel drive; choice of four-speed manual gearbox with overdrive, or three-speed automatic, also with overdrive. Top gear mph at 1000 rpm: 25 (OD); 28.6 (auto. OD).

Suspension: Front, independent, MacPherson struts; coil springs and telescopic dampers. Anti-roll bar. Rear, live axle located by pivoted sub-frame and trailing arms; coil springs and telescopic dampers. Anti-roll bar.

Steering: Rack and pinion with power assistance.

Brakes: Discs front, and rear, servo-assisted.

Tyres: 195/60 HR 15; 6 in rim.

Dimensions: Length 4785 mm (188 in), width 1761 mm (69.3 in), height 1410 mm (55.5 in), wheelbase 2770 mm (109 in).

Unladen weight: 1330 kg (2930 lb).

Performance: Maximum speed, 124 mph. 0 to 60 mph, 8.5 sec. Fuel consumption, 28.0 mpg (at constant 75 mph) auto; 28.5, manual.

Features: Roomy, comfortable and quiet saloon. Generous standard equipment including air conditioning, electric window lifts and door mirror adjustment, central locking, and heating for front seats. Alloy wheels.